*Saudi Arabia
and Israel*

Saudi Arabia and Israel

THE SINFUL PROXIMITY

GEW Intelligence Unit
HICHEM KAROUI (ED.)

The Voice of the Mediterranean (France)/ Global East-West (London)

Copyright © 2024 by GEW Intelligence Unit

Research Director and Editor: Dr. Hichem Karoui

GEW Reports and Analyses (g-ew.com)

This book relies on two kinds of sources. Some are open sources, such as scholarly references and publicly available media, cited after every chapter. Besides, the GEW Intelligence Unit has relied on direct information from non-open sources, mainly in the USA, Europe, and other countries. While we cannot unveil these sources that leaked confidential matters to us, we made the choice of any researcher or political analyst gathering information from different sources and bringing it into the report. We thought it necessary to put everything we had on the table and let the reader be free to interpret.

Not all opinions and information presented in this book represent GEW Reports and Analyses (g-ew.com) or its Director.

Publisher: Global East-West (London).

All rights reserved. No part of this book may be reproduced in any manner whatsoever without written permission except in the case of brief quotations embodied in critical articles and reviews.

First Printing, 2024

Contents

I	The Current State of Unofficial Israeli-Saudi Relations	1
Sources and References		25
II	Introduction	31
III	Historical Background	44
Sources and References		62
IV	Present Relationships	64
Sources and References		84
V	Secret Contacts and Covert Cooperation	86
Sources and References		103
VI	Regional Conflicts and Struggles	105
Sources and References		126
VII	Prospects	128
Sources and References		147
VIII	Implications for Global Diplomacy	149
Sources and References		166
IX	Societal Impact and Domestic Perspectives	168
Sources and References		189

X	Human Rights Concerns and Ethical Dilemmas	191
Sources and References		210
XI	Conclusion	212

I

The Current State of Unofficial Israeli-Saudi Relations

PREFACE BY HICHEM KAROUI

1. Background of Israeli-Saudi Relations

The Gulf War and the Oslo Accords marked two watershed moments in Israeli-Saudi ties. The First Gulf War strained relations between Saudi Arabia and the United States, which supported Israel during the fight. Due to this strained relationship, Saudi Arabia officially condemned Israel's refusal to attend the 1991 Madrid Conference, which Saudi Arabia saw as an opportunity to isolate Israel in an Arab-US negotiation further. As a result of this censure,

Israel was barred from participating in the conference's joint sessions, which included multilateral talks. These sessions aimed to form working groups to address various Middle Eastern concerns, with each group preferably containing representatives from Arab governments and Israel. Although the Madrid framework was never necessary for any peace process, Saudi Arabia hailed Israel's absence as a win and has repeatedly attempted to utilise this format to isolate Israel further. (Rynhold, Yaari, 2020)(Nawaz)

From a historical standpoint, no Saudi King has officially met an Israeli prime, let alone engaged in good public discourse regarding relations with Israel. During UN meetings, Saudi and Israeli diplomats undoubtedly acknowledged one another's presence; in such a close-knit organisation, it is impossible to ignore another country's representative fully. However, this has resulted in relatively little informal cooperation between the two countries. Rumours have circulated in the past that Saudi and Israeli leaders met secretly to discuss relations, most notably following the Gulf War. Both sides have continuously denied any such allegations, and actual diplomatic contacts are almost non-existent. (Yaari2020)(Niu, Wu, 2021).

Historically, Saudi Arabia and Israel have had a distant and frosty relationship. Saudi Arabia has led the Arab world's diplomatic efforts to isolate Israel within the international community. Saudi Arabia is considered one of the last Arab countries to refuse to recognise Israel. However, the Arab Spring and subsequent revolutions in the area have raised Saudi Arabia's uneasiness and highlighted the probability that Iran may pose a more significant threat to the kingdom than Israel. This has resulted in a minor shift in Saudi policy towards Israel, based on the belief that the enemy of my enemy is my friend. (Beck, 2020)(Rynhold, Yaari, 2020).

1.1 Historical context

The Kingdom of Saudi Arabia has engaged in various foreign policy initiatives, including diplomatic relations with other countries and engagement in the Arab-Israeli conflict. One of the most intriguing aspects of the kingdom's foreign policy is its unofficial relationship with Israel. Actually, the Kingdom of Saudi Arabia and the State of Israel have never maintained formal diplomatic relations. However, both parties had numerous interactions, some of which occurred behind closed doors. Saudi Arabia's inclination to engage with Israel is motivated by a desire to resolve the Palestinian issue. Both parties have met multiple times to explore ways to bring peace to the Levant, with the Saudi plan being the main focus of their discussions. These sessions were conducted in secret, away from the media's notice. Typically, the Saudi king and the Israeli Prime Minister meet with a delegation of officials. However, on one occasion, the Saudis met in secret with former Israel Defence Minister Ariel Scheinmann, who is in charge of the IOF's scenario and strategy. However, the most famous interaction between a Saudi regent and an Israeli prime minister occurred in 1998, when Ariel Sharon met with the late King Fahd on Al Jazeera. This interaction, despite being harshly criticised by Arab nations and Israelis themselves, demonstrated that the Saudis and Israelis desire to find a peaceful solution in the Levant. However, there were other meetings besides those behind the curtain. Saudi and Israeli officials had met multiple times during UN meetings. Typically, one party would seek the assistance of a mediator to facilitate a meeting with the opposing party. And, during UN meetings, the United States is the greatest place to find an Arab-Israeli mediator. For example, former Israeli Prime Minister Ehud Barak met with Saudi Foreign Affairs Minister Saud Al Faisal during the UN General Assembly in 2002. Nabil Sha'at, the Palestinian National Authority's foreign affairs minister, disrupted the meeting. The Israelis' most recent encounters were with King Abdullah. For example, Israeli Livni met with Abdullah in 2008, and Netanyahu and Abdullah met in Amman on June 25, 2012. Both talks focused on the Palestinian dilemma, with Israeli delegates asking if Saudi Arabians would be ready to work with an Israeli initiative to find a solution. Despite the numerous interactions, Saudi assistance in finding a solution for the Levant continues to be highly criticised by its Arab neighbours and Palestinians. Prince Turki Al Faisal resigned from his position as Saudi Intelligence chief in protest over Saudi cooperation with Israel. (Yaari, 2020; Rahman; Kibrik et al., 2021).

1.2 Meetings behind the curtains or during the UN sessions

One alternative to high-level direct meetings between state officials is meetings during UN sessions or events involving people not holding official government posts. One instance of this occurred in October 2009 with a UN-sponsored event in New York intended to raise funds for the UN agency aiding Palestinian refugees. Then, Saudi Foreign Minister Prince Saud and Israeli Deputy Foreign Minister Danny Ayalon attended the event. According to an American present at the event, Prince Saud and Danny Ayalon had a direct meeting and lengthy conversation involving the Israeli-Palestinian conflict and the Iranian threat. This account was verified by other diplomatic sources and reported in the Israeli media. Another noteworthy meeting at a non-official level was reported to occur in 2016 with a delegation from the Saudi-backed Gulf States visiting a synagogue in the United States and having a significant meeting with Israeli officials to discuss the common perceived threat from Iran. These types of meetings are easier to verify due to attendees not needing to hide their identities and may perhaps be an important area to monitor in assessing the future of relations between the Saudi and Israeli states. (Moniruzzaman, 2024)(Eilam, 2022). According to diplomatic sources, media accounts, and independent public declarations, direct contacts between Saudi and Israeli officials are uncommon and usually occur outside the public view. According to reports, Israeli and Saudi intelligence leaders met in Egypt in 2006 to discuss their shared perception of Iran's threat. This is an uncommon meeting between high-ranking officials from the two states on mainland Arab territory. The British Sunday Times stated that another such high-level direct meeting took place in Italy in December 2014 with Saudi cabinet and intelligence officials, as well as the then-Israeli National Security Advisor, Yossi Cohen. A similar claimed incident occurred in November 2014 in Paris, when Saudi officials met with an Israeli Foreign Ministry representative. These behind-the-scenes encounters have the potential to alter the relationship between the two governments significantly, but verification is difficult due to individuals involved's denial and secrecy. (Mäkelä, 2023)(Ferziger, Bahgat, 2020)(kibrik et al., 2021).

1.3 Key events and milestones

The Oslo phase (1993-1995) might be seen as the forerunner of the bilateral partnership. First, Saudi Arabia acknowledged the efforts of the Israelis and the PLO, and second, the killing of Israeli Prime Minister Yitzhak Rabin, with whom the Saudis had developed close personal ties. During this time, Saudis and Israelis engaged in more informal interactions in order to foster mutual trust and set the groundwork for future collaboration. According to reports, Israeli-Saudi collaboration on intelligence and security issues intensified as the peace process progressed. This includes facilitating discussions between the two sides and Israeli training of Palestinian security personnel from 1997 to 1999, as well as the

Camp David negotiations in 2000. This period was not without Arab-Israeli conflicts (for example, the Gulf War and Lebanon in 2006), and Saudi Arabia distanced itself from Israel during times of crisis. Prince Bandar bin Sultan al-Saud, Saudi Ambassador to the United States, met with Prime Minister Ariel Sharon during the 2002-2003 Intifada, which received widespread attention. The Saudi activities at the 2002 Arab League Beirut Summit and the 2007 Mecca Agreement (between Hamas and Fatah) were regarded as attempts to mediate issues between Israel and the Arabs. (Niu, Wu, 2021)(Yaari 2020)(Rynhold and Yaari, 2021).

2. Implications of the Gaza War on Israeli-Saudi Relations

During the 2008-2009 Gaza War, at which time Israel was in official talks with Saudi Arabia over the Arab Peace Initiative, the kingdom called for the immediate cessation of Israeli military action against Palestinian civilians and urged the international community to step in and prevent Israel from further bloodshed. While not explicitly condemning Israel, a statement from King Abdullah on January 4, 2009, conveyed Saudi Arabia's view on a link between the war and the peace process, and his April 22, 2009, meeting with US President Obama led to a push for a permanent end to the Arab-Israeli conflict and a comprehensive two-state solution for the Israeli-Palestinian conflict. The Saudis appeared to have been disappointed at Israel's refusal to halt settlement expansion as a result of US pressure, and on November 3, 2010, an Al-Arabiya interview with Prince Turki al-Faisal saw a touting of the Saudi-Hamas rapprochement and a push for Palestinian national unity – things which would not have sat comfortably with the US or Israel. Simulation of a December 2010 war incident in the Persian Gulf, where Israeli aircraft were reported to have overflown Saudi territory amidst talks of an attack on Iran, saw a hypothetical Saudi response to have an open confrontation with Israel, and whether in simulation or reality, it is clear that any future Israeli military actions seen to threaten Gulf security or communal interests will not go unnoticed with Saudi Arabia. (Louwerse2020)(Pradhan, 2023)

> The ongoing Gaza War has significant implications for Israeli-Saudi relations, affecting both the potential for normalization between the two countries and the broader geopolitical landscape in the Middle East. Here are the key points:
>
> 1. Stalled Normalization Efforts
> - Before the outbreak of the Gaza War on October 7, 2023, there were indications that Saudi Arabia and Israel were moving towards normalization of relations, potentially joining the Abraham Accords, which already include the UAE, Bahrain, Morocco, and Sudan. However, the conflict has led to a pause in these discussions.
> - Saudi Arabia has made it clear that any normalization with Israel must be contingent upon significant progress towards the establishment of a Palestinian state with East Jerusalem as its capital. This stance has been reiterated in light of the Gaza conflict, with Saudi officials emphasizing the need for a resolution to the Palestinian issue before proceeding with any formal ties with Israel.
>
> 2. Impact of the Gaza War

- The war has intensified Saudi Arabia's focus on the Palestinian statehood issue. The kingdom has been vocal about its conditions for normalization, which include the cessation of Israeli aggression in Gaza and a clear path to the establishment of a Palestinian state.
- The conflict has also affected public and official attitudes within Saudi Arabia towards Israel. Reports suggest a hardening of positions, with increased support for the Palestinians and greater skepticism towards normalization without substantial concessions from Israel.

3. Geopolitical Realignments
- The war has potentially shifted the dynamics of regional alliances. Saudi Arabia's firm stance on Palestinian statehood as a precondition for normalization with Israel could influence other Arab states' policies and affect the overall feasibility of broader Arab-Israeli normalization.
- Additionally, the conflict has exposed the limits of U.S. influence in the region, with Saudi Arabia and other Arab states increasingly willing to assert their positions independently of American preferences.

4. Saudi Arabia's Role in Post-War Scenarios
- Discussions have emerged about Saudi Arabia's potential role in the administration of Gaza post-conflict. Proposals have been made for Saudi involvement in governance or reconstruction efforts, although these are contingent on a broader political settlement.
- Saudi Arabia's leadership in pushing for a unified Arab stance on the Palestinian issue and its active diplomacy in international forums highlight its central role in shaping the post-war landscape.

5. Long-term Implications
   - The prolongation of the Gaza War without a clear path to resolution could further complicate Saudi-Israeli relations, making normalization more difficult to achieve in the near term.
   - The situation underscores the complexity of balancing strategic interests with public sentiment and religious considerations, particularly given Saudi Arabia's status as the custodian of Islam's holiest sites.

In summary, the Gaza War has significantly impacted the trajectory of Israeli-Saudi relations, injecting greater uncertainty into the normalization process and highlighting the centrality of the Palestinian issue in any future agreements. The conflict has not only stalled potential diplomatic breakthroughs but has also reinforced the importance of addressing Palestinian statehood in the context of regional peace and stability.

2.1 Impact on diplomatic ties

The initial ambiguity and noncommittal response of foreign ministers in the Arab League and the Organization of Islamic Cooperation (OIC) is reflected in the early response of the Saudi state. It was brought to light that Israel had informally engaged a number of Gulf States, including Saudi, in 2012-2013 with the aim of building an alliance to counteract the threat of a nuclear Iran. Although details of these talks were initially undisclosed, the revelation of these discussions led to the Saudi foreign ministry indicating no formal complaints about these talks until after the onset of the Gaza conflict. It was stated that Saudi would only complain if these talks were linked to the Gaza conflict. These complaints and a demand for Israeli concessions to the PA were later conveyed through the US. The conditions of a Saudi break in future relations with Israel were made explicitly clear by Prince Turki in an interview on July 27th, who outlined a five-point plan including the suspension of all oil sales to Israel and only Saudi Arabia recognizing and offering legitimacy to Israel, effectively cutting all contact between Israel and Saudi Arabia. This unparalleled public transparency in Saudi-Israel relations is indicative of the severity of the Gaza war on official Saudi perceptions of Israel. It is clear that the intensity of the conflict has forced Saudi diplomats to acknowledge Israeli actions as a direct threat to Saudi interests, in contrast to previous instances where external pressures influenced Saudi reactions. (Beck, 2020)(Niu and Wu, 2021).

2.2 Shared concerns and interests

Saudi concern over Iran has been demonstrated by the alleged offer of the use of its airspace to the Israeli Air Force for strikes on Iranian nuclear facilities. It is inconclusive from reports whether any such request was made during the period of the Gaza War itself, though confirmation of the offer came during the subsequent year. However, Saudi Public Affairs Adviser Adel al-Jubeir told reporters that "the Saudi government has made it clear that it will not stand idly by and will take the necessary steps to protect its national security from the harm caused by the Iranian nuclear program." This is a sentiment shared by Israel, and whether or not the offer was on the table during the Gaza War, it shows that there is a high level of understanding between the two states on this issue. Middle East commentator Simon Henderson added Saudi concern over Iranian influence in Gaza via its proxy Hezbollah as a motive for the offer.

He noted that whilst the Saudi government had made a public call for a ceasefire in the war, the more receptive portrayal of the idea in the Saudi press revealed disapproval of Egyptian and Turkish mediation efforts which were seen as favorable to Hamas. In short, parallel Saudi and Israeli interests have led to Saudi overtures that would have once been unthinkable. (Cordesman and Toukan, 2022)(Cook and Indyk, 2022).

According to a popular axiom in IR theory, "an enemy's enemy is a friend." Analysis of Israel-Saudi relations during the course of the Gaza War may add a corollary to this, that is, "a friend's vocal condemnation of an enemy may be indistinguishable from tacit support." It is clear that both states share grave concerns over the rising power of Iran, the expansion of radical Islamist movements, and a US policy of military disengagement in the Middle East. Whilst Saudi Arabia is unlikely to alter its essential policy of hostility to the Jewish state, there are indicators that the implicit alliance between the two states based on common enemies is still alive during this period. (Beck, 2020)(Niu and Wu, 2021)(Rynhold and Yaari, 2020).

2.3 Potential for cooperation or conflict

Israel and Saudi Arabia both have interests in reshaping the Middle East order and have cooperated in attempts to stymie the regional weight of Iran and Syria. Now, it is said that there is no potential for future Saudi cooperation. Recent histories of conflict and contest have since taken a backseat as the two governments share a sense of vulnerability to violent non-state Islamism and now Palestinian nationalism, resulting in the muting of Saudi verbal hostilities towards Israel and the emergence of common strategic discourse. Though the Saudi government does not want to be seen as appeasing Israel, their 'de facto' recognition of Israel's right to defend itself and its interests at the expense of Palestinian interest is seen to be close to a quid-pro-quo understanding outlined in the road-map but with a focus on the second phase. This has become evident in what was the strongest Bush administration in condemning Israel in its military ventures in the region. The recent war in Gaza has seen a minor re-emergence in public discord between the two nations. The Saudis have criticized the use of excessive force and collective punishment in Gaza and demanded more decisive international action to disarm Israel. Adversely, Israel has seen its incursion as a success in weakening the Hamas apparatus and thus decreasing the threat of Islamist attacks and has rejected ceasefire calls, which it pretended would only help stabilise Hamas' rule in the Palestinian territories. In a recent interview with Elaph, a UK news site with strong Saudi ties, Defense Minister Barak has said that there can be no comprehensive peace deal with Israel until there is unity between the conflicting Palestinian territories, thus indicating Israel's disinterest with the current Saudi peace plan. (Rynhold and Yaari, 2021)(Braimah2024)(Rynhold and Yaari, 2020)(Fantina, 2023).

3. Public Perception and Reactions

The US and international media are not the only ones reporting on this conflict. Part of the Arab media has been more strident in its criticism of Israel. The message being presented is that this is an all-out Israeli war against the Palestinian people. Although this is in fact the stated goal of the Israeli occupation army, this context has been omitted in most Western media reports. The authoritarian Arab regimes who have been threatened by or critical of Hamas have also been involved in cognitive warfare against Israel to divert attention and provide themselves with some protection against backlash from their home populations. This is primarily why the Saudis have been allowed to act so hypocritically in giving their tacit support to Israel. (Qawariq2020)(AR, 2024).

Yet, there is broad consensus that the Palestinian media strategy has been successful.

There is little question that the Israel-Gaza crisis is the most difficult public relations test Israel has faced. During the first 10 days of the military offensive, 675 stories appeared in the American media. Of these, 206 were headlines on the front page and 74 appeared on the front page of The New York Times. These headlines and stories focused on a number of issues including the capture of two Israeli soldiers, the killing of Palestinians and bombings of Palestinian infrastructure in Gaza. Note that the total number of stories released in America concerning the "war on terrorism" in the two weeks following September 11th was 131. This is no accident. The public relations campaign launched by the Palestinians was timed to maximize the impact of their messages. This goal was to make metaphorical "noise" in the hopes that they could reach parity in the information war and force the international community to intervene. (Rusiecki, 2020)(Kargar and Rid, 2024)(Lewandowsky et al., 2020).

3.1 Media coverage and public discourse

There is a particularly interesting finding in an article from the Saudi publication, the Arab News, printed on Jan 6, 2009 (following the ceasefire), entitled "Israel and Hamas both claim victory in Gaza War." In what is a rarity for Saudi media, the story gives considerable coverage to both sides of the conflict, and while the article is largely made up of Hamas rhetoric, the simple fact that Israeli views were given consideration was significant. This was fueled by the belief of many Saudi leaders that some of Hamas' actions had undermined the Palestinian position and, by extension, Saudi interests in the region. (Zghoul, 2022)(Tivadar, 2021).

During the war in Gaza, there seems to be an Israeli perception that Saudi media coverage was biased. However, little factual evidence to support these general assumptions can be identified. Furthermore, the perception that Saudi media has not covered the war in significant detail is incorrect. A content analysis of the English language daily Arab News reveals 117 articles were published during the period of the war. An analysis of the Saudi English language daily, the Saudi Gazette, reveals Gazan war-related stories were positioned on the front page of the printed publication on every day of the war, bar one. However, it must be acknowledged that the Saudi Arabian media is not renowned for its open and free journalism, with various levels of censorship practiced. In this way, it was difficult to gauge sentiment, and although there was no outright anti-Gaza rhetoric, some media outlets appeared to favor Israeli security concerns over Palestinian welfare. (Elhosary, 2024)(Alsaba, 2023).

3.2 Government statements and official positions

Israeli government statements have overall been of Israeli commitment to continue attacks in Gaza until all tunnels from Gaza into Israel have been destroyed and Israeli citizens are safe from resistance attacks. There has been some disagreement in the Israeli parliament and calls for a cease-fire too soon. This comes as reports suggest that Israeli Occupation Force tactics and equipment seem to indicate that the IOF may have expected a much smaller ground invasion and are unprepared for the tasks at hand. (Schleifer and Ansbacher)(Zanotti and Sharp, 2023).

One does not need to be a supporter of Hamas to condemn the Israeli genocide in Gaza, but one needs only to be human. An example of this is the call of US President Obama to sever all US military aid to Israel following the bombing of the Gaza power plant. Although some US politicians are in disagreement, there have been no radical anti-Israeli statements from leaders of countries with strong diplomatic ties with Israel, such as Egypt and Jordan, who continue to discuss cease-fire resolutions with Israel and Palestinian authorities. (Obaid, 2020)(Kassem2021).

When the conflict began, it was reported that the overall public opinion in Saudi Arabia was that Israel was not a serious concern for the Kingdom, despite the ongoing terror acts from extremists such as Al-Qaeda. This was an alleged statement from the Saudi King, and many in the Arab world feel that the sale of US military arms to Saudi Arabia and other Arab states is an attempt to push further unity between Israel and those in the Arab world ready to forget that Palestine is still under occupation. (Pollock2021)(Quamar, 2020)(Rynhold and Yaari, 2020).

3.3 Public opinion polls and surveys

Our research results do indicate a strong opposition among Saudis towards normalization with Israel and a significant shift in public opinion in favor of Hamas following the recent conflict. Here are the findings :

1. Opposition to Normalization and Support for Hamas: A significant majority of Saudis oppose normalization with Israel, with recent polls showing that 96% believe Arab countries should cut all ties with Israel in protest against its actions in Gaza (i24news.tv Poll)(middle east monitor poll)(New York Times, 2023)(Washington Institute)(Middle East Eye). Additionally, there has been a notable increase in positive opinions of Hamas among Saudis, rising from 10% to 40% (i24news.tv)(Middle East monitor)(Middle East eye.)

2. Perception of the Conflict: The search results indicate that a large majority of Saudis view the conflict as a victory for Palestinians and the Arab world, with 91% holding this view(i24news.tv) (Washington Institute). There is also a widespread perception that Israel appears weakened by the conflict (i24news.tv).

3. Support for Armed Struggle: While the research results show increased support for Hamas and strong opposition to normalization with Israel, they do not specifically mention the percentage of Saudis who believe that "armed struggle is the best means for liberating all of historic Palestine." The results do show significant opposition to Israeli actions and a shift towards more supportive views of Palestinian resistance (i24news.tv) (Middle East Monitor) (Middle East Eye).

In summary, the research results do confirm a shift in Saudi public opinion towards more supportive views of Hamas and a strong opposition to normalization with Israel.

These figures represent a huge gap between the official Saudi position on the situation and the general public's opinion. With two-thirds of Saudis claiming that their general understanding of international affairs has increased during the recent conflict, there has been a call for Saudis to take a more direct role in influencing government policy. Though no official diplomatic relations with Israel exist, this has led to speculation that Saudi policy on the conflict and Palestine may soon be coming under reform, with the goal of a Saudi peace initiative. This has been noted by Prince Turki Al-Faisal, former ambassador to the United States and United Kingdom and former director general of the Saudi Intelligence Agency, who has called for Saudis to play a direct role in the Israel-Palestine conflict. His statements demonstrate that the Saudi public is pressuring the government to change its current role in the conflict. He is quoted as saying, "if the Palestinians are going to sit and negotiate with the Israelis, I hope that they can count on the support of the entire Arab and Islamic world for incorporating a substantial Saudi role in the peace process."

3.4 Role of social media

The term social media includes all means of mass communication that can be manipulated and intended to be shared among many people. This is a particularly significant medium during any war. The fact that the war began only one year after the disengagement from Gaza created an atmosphere of criticism and disdain for government policymaking. The public perception was that the government was caving into international pressure and committing acts of cowardice counter to their party platforms of increasing strength and security. Many took to forums and blogs to vent their frustration and criticize the government. Often, these expressions were cited in the mainstream media and helped create an image of a distrustful and disillusioned public. Another social medium in which people expressed opposition to the war was through political cartoons. These were widely circulated and often depicted the IOF with negative connotations and its war against Hamas as fruitless and immoral. This was particularly damaging when some of these cartoons were picked up by international media and used as depictions of the war. The publicized events during the war and how they were depicted helped significantly sway public opinion, mainly against the government and military actions. (Duygu, 2023).

4. Future Prospects and Challenges

A comprehensive analysis of the current state of Israel-Saudi relations in light of the Gaza war is crucial in predicting future trends and challenges. Theoretical approaches in political science and international relations, such as realism, liberalism, and constructivism, can provide insight into the future prospects of these relations. The complexity of the current relationship between the two countries, which are not openly at war with each other but do not have formal diplomatic relations, creates a unique and interesting case study. The challenge they face in their relationship with each other, especially in the aftermath of the Gaza war, is to keep the relationship resilient without increasing tension to the point of becoming political enemies. Israel has already created a powerful enemy in Iran and likely does not seek another one at this point. Saudi Arabia also does not want to complicate the situation with another conflict with Israel. Western observers believe that the Gaza war benefits both Israel and Saudi Arabia to some extent because of their mutual disdain for Hamas. This common interest would force the two countries to consider cooperation. However, Israel's rebellion against the international community during the war may lead to a slightly more isolated position than Saudi Arabia, which has been under intense pressure from sister Arab states and the international community to take action against Israel. Israel's suspicions of increased Saudi aid to Hamas during the war could act as a stumbling block to potential future cooperation. An interesting example of this was Israel's seizure of a ship in the Red Sea containing Iranian weapons allegedly destined for Hamas. The ship actually belonged to Iran's Revolutionary Guard, yet Israel declared it a Saudi ship in an attempt to discredit Saudi Arabia. The move shows Israel's concern about the more moderate approach Saudi

Arabia has recently taken to relations between Israel and Hamas. Although the future is highly uncertain, some Western observers still claim that the most mutually beneficial situations will lead the two countries towards greater cooperation, and in the event of another regional conflict, it is not unlikely that the two countries will decide to form a tacit alliance. However, the nature of this relationship will remain a delicate balance between realpolitik and cautious interaction due to various pressures that may limit the extent of cooperation.

4.1 The weight of the Zionist continual aggression on the Saudi officials

In analyzing the impasse in Israeli-Saudi relations, the Saudi-Israeli peace plan, anonymously authored and allegedly backed by Prince Bandar, is often cited as a starting point for unofficial relations. The plan suggested full recognition of Israel by all Arab states in exchange for a withdrawal to the 1967 borders and a Palestinian state. Interestingly, the plan was not completely rejected by Israel, but its details and timing made it unrealistic. Given Israel's position on the right of return of Palestinian refugees and its unwillingness to relinquish all occupied territory, the plan was essentially a peace offer to Arabs and Palestinians who continue to make concessions before getting peace based on a just final settlement. Herein lies the problem for Israel-Saudi relations. The Saudis feel that subsequent events have proven this interpretation correct. (Radcliffe et al., 2023).

4.2 Possibilities for reconciliation or escalation

while there is no solution looming for the Palestinians

Despite the common enmity towards one another, the increasing cooperation between Israel and the Saudis has signalled that there may be a point in time where Saudi officials can no longer withstand the pressure applied by the Israeli government to cut unofficial ties. With the visit of Olmert to Riyadh, the first high-profile meeting between an Israeli and Saudi official, it was evident that the Saudis felt increasing pressure that, at present, the benefits of maintaining relations with Israel were beginning to outweigh the cost. Despite Olmert's calls for Saudi help in the release of Israeli soldiers held by Hezbollah and Hamas, the Saudi King stated that Saudi support for Israel hinges on its withdrawal from Arab lands. Symbolic of this increasing cooperation are the alleged secret meetings between Israeli and Saudi officials. A senior Israeli official disclosed one such meeting stated that a senior Saudi official came to Israel to meet his Israeli counterpart about two years ago. With increasing pressure being put on them by Saudi-Bush diplomatic efforts to assist the ailing US steps in Iraq, which incidentally involved talks with Iran, it was rumored that the meeting was to ask for Israeli assurance that they would not disrupt US domination of Iraq or attempt to stem Iranian influence in the country, in return for Saudi efforts to begin to warm official ties with Israel. The Gaza war also cited Israeli claims that Saudi intelligence services contacted them and offered assistance in preventing further weapon smuggling into Gaza. Although such a move would be unpopular to the Saudi populace, it has not yet been substantiated by any Saudi officials. Intelligence minister Ephraim Sneh stated in an interview that he had received messages that showed Saudi willingness to help.

4.3 Role of regional dynamics and alliances

During the July 2014 Israel-Gaza conflict, it was evident that the Israeli siege and bombing campaign was met with relatively moderate opposition from key Arab states such as Saudi Arabia. The overture of a potential Israeli ground invasion was given de facto assent by Egypt and Saudi Arabia. However, immense pressure from the US and key European allies and widespread public dissent ultimately caused many Arab regimes to alter their stance. It is critical to realize that the Zionist-Saudi relationship exists in a complex regional framework where both states are attempting to navigate in a time of significant geopolitical uncertainty. The 'Arab Spring' saw the removal of key allies for Saudi Arabia, such as Ben-Ali in Tunisia and Mubarak in Egypt. It saw an unprecedented level of public mobilization and an increase of regional support for political Islam. Saudi Arabia viewed these developments as an existential threat, given that they could inspire similar movements to question the legitimacy of the House of Saud directly. Hence, Saudi Arabia believed that the primary issue of the Middle East became one of instability and uncertainty, and this had a direct effect on the Saudi decision to seek a solution to its 'Palestinian problem'.

However, if some pretend that the Saudis did nothing to pressure Israel in the 2024 War on Gaza, this is not entirely accurate. The research results indicate that Saudi Arabia has been actively involved in diplomatic efforts and public statements that express opposition to Israel's actions and support for the Palestinian cause, particularly during the 2024 conflict.

Diplomatic Efforts and Public Statements

1. Saudi Leadership in Diplomacy: Saudi Arabia has been at the

forefront of diplomatic efforts to address the conflict. For instance, the kingdom hosted a meeting with key Arab states to forge a common position on how to end Israel's war on Hamas, emphasizing the need for an immediate and full ceasefire and the removal of obstacles to the entry of aid into Gaza(Bloomberg, February 2024).

2. Public Opposition to Israeli Actions: Saudi Arabia has publicly voiced its opposition to Israeli actions in Gaza. The Saudi government has issued statements denouncing the displacement of Palestinians and the targeting of civilians by Israeli forces. These statements reflect a strong stance against what Riyadh perceives as aggressive and disproportionate actions by Israel(FRANCE 24, October 2023).

3. Calls for Arab and International Action: Saudi Arabia has called for immediate action from Arab countries and the international community to address the situation in Gaza. This includes breaking all diplomatic and economic ties with Israel in protest against its military actions(Washington Institute, Dec 21, 2023). The kingdom has also been active in rallying international support for a ceasefire and a resolution to the conflict that respects the rights of the Palestinian people (Bloomberg, February 2024).

4. Media and Public Sentiment: The Saudi public and media have expressed significant opposition to Israel's actions. There has been widespread condemnation across social media and in public statements by officials, reflecting a strong sentiment against the Israeli military campaign(The New Arab, November 2023).

Comparison with 2014

When Saudi Arabia's response in 2024 is compared to its stance during the 2014 conflict, it appears that Riyadh has taken a more active and vocal role in opposing Israeli actions and supporting the Palestinian cause in the recent conflict. This shift could be attributed to several factors, including changes in regional dynamics, international pressure, and a more assertive Saudi foreign policy under current leadership.

In summary, while there may be perceptions that Saudi Arabia has not done enough to oppose or contain Israel's response to the October 7 operation, the evidence from the search results suggests that the kingdom has been actively involved in diplomatic efforts and public declarations against Israel's actions in Gaza. These efforts indicate a significant level of engagement and opposition to the Israeli military campaign, contrasting with the impression that Saudi Arabia remained passive or uninvolved.

Last but not least

This book relies on two kinds of sources. Some are open sources, such as scholarly references and publicly available media, cited after every chapter. Besides, the GEW Intelligence Unit has relied on direct information from non-open sources, mainly in the USA, Europe, and other countries. While we cannot unveil these sources that leaked confidential matters to us, we made the choice of any researcher or political analyst gathering information from different sources and bringing it into the report. We thought it necessary to put everything we had on the table and let the reader be free to interpret.

Therefore, not all opinions and information presented in this book represent GEW Reports and Analyses (g-ew.com) or its Director.

Sources and References

Rynhold, J. and Yaari, M. "The transformation of Saudi-Israeli relations." Israel Affairs (2020). academia.edu

Nawaz, A. "Normalisation of Relations Between Saudi Arabia & Israel: Assessment of Critical Aspects." researchgate.net . researchgate.net

Yaari, Michal. "Israel and Saudi Arabia: On the way to normalization." Israel's relations with Arab countries: The unfulfilled potential (2020): 57-71. mitvim.org.il

Niu, S. and Wu, T. "Changes and trends in the current relations between saudi arabia and israel." Asian Journal of Middle Eastern and Islamic Studies (2021). [HTML]

Beck, M. "The aggravated struggle for regional power in the Middle East: American allies Saudi Arabia and Israel versus Iran." Global Policy (2020). sdu.dk

Rahman, O. "The emergence of GCC-Israel relations in a changing Middle East." Brookings Institution. Washington . mecouncil.org

Kibrik, R., Goren, N., and Kahana-Dagan, M. "Israel's Relations with Arab Countries: The Unfulfilled Potential." (2021). mitvim.org.il

Moniruzzaman, M. "The Arab–Israeli Diplomatic Normalization and Its Implications for South and Southeast Asian Muslim Countries." Arab-Israel Normalisation of Ties: Global Perspectives (2024). researchgate.net

Eilam, E. "Israel's National Security, the Arab Position, and Its Complicated Relations with the United States." (2022). [HTML]

Mäkelä, J. "Security Elites in Egypt and Jordan after the Arab Spring: A Case Study on Securocracies' Role on National Security, Domestic Power Politics, Regional Order and ...." (2023). doria.fi

Ferziger, J. H. and Bahgat, G. "Israel's growing ties with the Gulf Arab states." (2020). atlanticcouncil.org

Rynhold, J. and Yaari, M. "The quiet revolution in Saudi-Israeli relations." Mediterranean Politics (2021). researchgate.net

Louwerse, Colter. "(Un) Limited Force: Regional Realignments, Israeli Operations, and the Security of Gaza." The Regional Order in the Gulf Region and the Middle East: Regional Rivalries and Security Alliances (2020): 217-257. [HTML]

Pradhan, B. "OCCUPATION VS. RESISTANCE." Arab Studies Quarterly (2023). scienceopen.com

Cordesman, A. H. and Toukan, A. "Iran and the Gulf Military Balance." (2022). psu.edu

Cook, S. A. and Indyk, M. "The Case for a New US-Saudi Strategic Compact." (2022). cfr.org

Braimah, Awaisu. "Killing to Cling to Power? The Dilemmas of Israeli Prime Minister." International Journal of Social Science Research and Review 7, no. 3 (2024): 205-218. ijssrr.com

Fantina, R. "Gaza and the Israeli War.." CounterPunch (2023). [HTML]

Qawariq, Rami. "Political and ideological tensions in Israel: a critical language analysis of news reporting of the 2014 Gaza war." An-Najah University Journal for Research-B (Humanities) 36, no. 7 (2020): 1531-1556. najah.edu

AR, M. F. "The News Media in Raising Conflicts Tension: A Critical Study Toward News Conflict Between Israel and Palestine." Tuturlogi: Journal of Southeast Asian Communication (2024). ub.ac.id

Jackson, H. M. "The New York Times distorts the Palestinian struggle: A case study of anti-Palestinian bias in US news coverage of the First and Second Palestinian Intifadas." Media . [HTML]

Yarchi, M. and Ayalon, A. "Fighting over the image: the Israeli– Palestinian conflict in the Gaza strip 2018– 19." Studies in Conflict & Terrorism (2023). [HTML]

Rusiecki, S. M. "The Greatest Crusade: D-Day, the Press, and the Making of an American Narrative." (2020). [HTML]

Kargar, S. and Rid, T. "Attributing Digital Covert Action: the curious case of WikiSaudileaks." Intelligence and National Security (2024). [HTML]

Lewandowsky, S., Jetter, M., and Ecker, U. K. H. "Using the president's tweets to understand political diversion in the age of social media." Nature communications (2020). nature.com

Zghoul, L. "Al-Jazeera English and BBC News coverage of the Gaza War 2008-9: A comparative examination." (2022). cardiff.ac.uk

Tivadar, L. M. "The Gaza Strip and the Israel-Hamas Conflict: From 2008 until Nowadays." Acta Musei Napocensis. Historica (2021). [HTML]

Elhosary, M. "When and Why Do Arabs Verify? Predicting Online News Verification Intention during the 2023 Gaza War." (2024). aucegypt.edu

Alsaba, M. R. "The Influence of The Abraham Accords on the Visual Coverage of the Israeli-Palestinian Conflict in Arab Media: A Comparative Analysis." (2023). aucegypt.edu

Schleifer, R. and Ansbacher, Y. "Deterrence in the Gaza Conflict: Hamas Case Study Analysis." DETERRENCE . oapen.org

Zanotti, J. and Sharp, J. M. "Israel and Hamas 2023 Conflict In Brief: Overview, US Policy, and Options for Congress." (2023). dtic.mil

Obaid, N. "The failure of the Muslim Brotherhood in the Arab World." (2020). [HTML]

Kassem, Samira K. "The Muslim Brotherhood's Influence and the Democratization of the Middle East." Res Publica-Journal of Undergraduate Research 26, no. 1 (2021): 11. iwu.edu

Pollock, David. "The Arab Spring Then and Now, through the Prism of Public Opinion." Strategic Assessment. Available online: https://www.washingtoninstitute.org/media/4419 (2021). inss.org.il

Quamar, M. M. "Changing regional geopolitics and the foundations of a rapprochement between Arab Gulf and Israel." Global Affairs (2020). [HTML]

Duygu, U. "Between politics and social media: examining domestic information operations through the Twitter controversy in Türkiye." (2023). sabanciuniv.edu

Radcliffe, D., Abuhmaid, H., and Mahliaire, N. "Social media in the Middle East 2022: A year in review." (2023). fipp.com

Online:

https://www.washingtoninstitute.org/policy-analysis/new-poll-sheds-light-saudi-views-israel-hamas-war

https://ip-quarterly.com/en/hamas-israel-and-cold-war-gulf

https://www.bloomberg.com/news/articles/2024-02-09/saudi-arabia-calls-for-palestine-state-with-allies-to-end-israel-hamas-war

https://www.aljazeera.com/news/2023/10/14/saudi-arabia-puts-israel-deal-on-ice-amid-war-engages-with-iran-report

https://www.dw.com/en/saudi-arabia-balancing-israel-ties-and-palestinian-solution/a-67943869

https://www.france24.com/en/middle-east/20231014-saudi-arabia-pauses-normalisation-talks-with-israel-amid-ongoing-war-with-hamas

https://www.newarab.com/analysis/how-saudi-arabia-approaching-israels-war-gaza

https://www.bbc.com/news/world-middle-east-67922238

https://www.iai.it/en/pubblicazioni/saudi-arabias-balancing-game-palestinian-cause-and-regional-leadership

https://responsiblestatecraft.org/iran-saudi-arabia-gaza/

https://www.scmp.com/week-asia/politics/article/3245232/fragile-saudi-peace-efforts-yemen-hamper-us-response-houthi-attacks-amid-israel-gaza-war

https://www.bbc.com/news/world-middle-east-67177684

https://www.amnesty.org/en/location/middle-east-and-north-africa/saudi-arabia/report-saudi-arabia/

https://www.arabnews.com/node/2393226/saudi-arabia

https://carnegieendowment.org/2023/10/13/arab-perspectives-on-middle-east-crisis-pub-90774

https://www.theguardian.com/world/2023/oct/08/hamas-attack-has-abruptly-altered-the-picture-for-middle-east-diplomacy

https://www.newarab.com/news/how-did-arab-states-react-hamas-attack-israel

https://www.washingtoninstitute.org/policy-analysis/international-reactions-hamas-attack-israel

https://www.aljazeera.com/news/2023/10/7/we-are-at-war-reactions-to-palestinian-hamas-surprise-attack-in-israel

https://russiancouncil.ru/en/blogs/a-khalfa/evolution-of-saudiisrael-relations-unveiling-the-shift-from-quiet-dipl/

https://www.atlanticcouncil.org/blogs/menasource/saudi-arabia-israel-two-state-gaza-normalization/

https://www.brookings.edu/articles/how-to-understand-israel-and-saudi-arabias-secretive-relationship/

https://amwaj.media/media-monitor/how-the-gaza-war-is-shaping-saudi-views-on-israel

https://www.aljazeera.com/news/2017/11/21/what-is-behind-the-covert-israeli-saudi-relations

https://responsiblestatecraft.org/iran-saudi-arabia-gaza/

https://www.foreignaffairs.com/middle-east/what-war-gaza-israel-means-saudi-arabia

https://www.al-monitor.com/originals/2024/02/saudi-arabia-says-no-relations-israel-recognition-palestinian-state-1967-borders

https://www.newarab.com/analysis/how-saudi-arabia-approaching-israels-war-gaza

https://en.wikipedia.org/wiki/Israel%E2%80%93Saudi_Arabia_relations

https://arabcenterdc.org/resource/saudi-arabia-may-be-taking-center-stage-in-post-gaza-peace/

https://www.reuters.com/world/middle-east/saudi-arabia-says-there-will-be-no-diplomatic-relations-with-israel-without-an-2024-02-07/

https://www.aljazeera.com/features/2023/12/11/israels-war-on-gaza-means-arab-normalisation-is-off-the-table-experts

https://www.dw.com/en/saudi-arabia-juggles-priorities-amid-israel-hamas-war/a-68278203

https://www.theguardian.com/world/2023/sep/21/saudi-arabia-getting-closer-to-normalising-relations-with-israel-crown-prince-says

https://www.bbc.com/news/world-middle-east-43632905

https://carnegieendowment.org/2020/10/15/what-would-happen-if-israel-and-saudi-arabia-established-official-relations-pub-82964

https://www.bloomberg.com/news/articles/2024-02-09/saudi-arabia-calls-for-palestine-state-with-allies-to-end-israel-hamas-war

https://foreignpolicy.com/2023/12/18/saudi-arabia-israel-gaza-mbs-leverage/

Introduction

Brief Overview of the Historical Context

The historical context of Saudi-Israeli relations is crucial to understanding the dynamics of their current interactions. Both countries emerged within the backdrop of a changing Middle East, shaped by the aftermath of colonial rule, regional conflicts, and shifting geopolitical alliances.

Saudi Arabia, founded in 1932, rose to prominence following the collapse of the Ottoman Empire and the subsequent division of the Middle East by Western powers. The establishment of the Kingdom of Saudi Arabia, under the leadership of Abdulaziz Al Saud, aimed to consolidate and unify the Arabian Peninsula. Initially, the kingdom focused primarily on domestic affairs, navigating the challenges of tribal politics, religious influence, and socio-economic development.

The birth of Israel in 1948 marked a significant turning point in the region's history. The Zionist movement, advocating for a Jewish homeland, gained momentum in the early 20th century. The United Nations Partition Plan of 1947 allocated land for both a Jewish state and an Arab state, leading to the establishment of Israel. However, this partition plan was rejected by neighboring Arab nations, prompting a series of conflicts and wars that would shape the region's dynamics for decades.

Importance of Analyzing Saudi-Israeli Relations

The Saudi-Israeli relationship holds profound implications for the Middle East, regional stability, and global diplomacy. As two influential actors in the region, their interactions have the potential to shape the geopolitical landscape. The historical and present-day connections between Saudi Arabia and Israel provide insights into their shared interests, regional struggles, and the prospects for future cooperation.

Throughout history, both countries have grappled with a complex web of strategic interests, ideological differences, and conflicting regional alliances. Saudi Arabia, as the "Custodian of the Two Holy Mosques" and the heartland of Islam, has maintained a cautious approach toward Israel, driven by concerns over Palestinian rights and the broader Arab-Israeli conflict. The Israeli occupation of Palestinian territories and the treatment of Palestinians continue to be significant factors in shaping Saudi Arabia's stance.

Israel, on the other hand, has focused on securing its existence in a predominantly hostile neighborhood, seeking strategic partnerships to counter regional threats. It has viewed Saudi Arabia as a potential ally due to shared concerns over Iran's regional ambitions, Hezbollah's rise in Lebanon, and the spread of radical Islamist groups. The convergence of strategic interests has fueled discreet cooperation between both countries, notably in the areas of intelligence sharing, counterterrorism efforts, and security cooperation.

Scope and Purpose of the Book

This book aims to provide an in-depth analysis of the Saudi-Israeli relationship, shedding light on the complexities, motivations, and implications of their interactions throughout history. By examining their historical background, current interactions, and covert cooperation that often remains hidden from the public eye, we can understand the progression of their relations from a cautious distance to more overt engagement.

One key aspect to explore is the impact of regional conflicts on the Saudi-Israeli relationship and the impact of the Palestinian plight on any future agreement. The Arab-Israeli wars, the Palestinian-Israeli conflict, and the rise of non-state actors such as Hezbollah and Hamas have all played a significant role in shaping their interactions. These conflicts have influenced Saudi Arabia's stance as it strives to balance its support for the Palestinian cause and its regional security considerations. The failure to resolve the Israeli-Palestinian conflict has perpetuated tensions and hindered the normalization of relations between the two nations.

Moreover, this book will delve into the potential for open diplomatic relations between Saudi Arabia and Israel. Is it possible in light of the ongoing conflict, where Israel – with the full support of the West – enjoy a liberty of mass-killing? Recent developments, including the Abraham Accords, have signaled a potential shift toward normalized relations. However, the UAE is not the land visited yearly by Muslim pilgrims. The UAE does not have an international religious weight nor a religious diplomacy. Examination of the drivers and obstacles to full diplomatic engagement provides insights into the future prospects of their bilateral relationship. The evolving dynamics of Saudi-Israeli relations impact other actors in the region, including Iran, Turkey, and the United States, making it crucial to analyze the broader implications for global diplomacy and regional stability.

Furthermore, societal impact, human rights concerns (the Genocide in Gaza), and ethical dilemmas associated with Saudi-Israeli relations cannot be ignored. The treatment of Palestinians, the Saudi-led war in Yemen, and the Israeli occupation of Palestinian territories all raise important moral and humanitarian considerations. This book will explore these issues, highlighting the challenges faced by both countries in balancing national interests and values with international expectations. It will also examine the influence of domestic and international pressures on their policies and decision-making processes.

Lastly, by examining the motivations, challenges, and outcomes of the Saudi-Israeli relationship, this book aims to extract key lessons and offer recommendations for future diplomatic engagement between these nations. Understanding the complexities of their relationship can guide policymakers, diplomats, and scholars in formulating strategies for fostering regional stability, conflict resolution, and mutual cooperation. It is vital to explore the potential roles of mediation, international initiatives, and multilateral approaches in bringing about long-term peace in the Middle East.

By exploring these dimensions, this book seeks to contribute to a deeper understanding of the Saudi-Israeli relationship, its impact on regional and global dynamics, and the opportunities and challenges it presents for future diplomacy. It aims to provide a comprehensive analysis of the historical, geopolitical, socio-cultural, and moral dimensions of this complex relationship, fostering greater awareness and informing future policy discussions.

A. BRIEF OVERVIEW OF THE HISTORICAL CONTEXT

Throughout history, the Middle East has been a region of great geopolitical significance and tensions, with Saudi-Israeli relations emerging as a crucial aspect within this complex landscape. To understand the dynamics between these two nations, it is essential to examine their historical context in greater depth.

1. Pre-Formation of Modern States The historical roots of Saudi-Israeli relations can be traced to the pre-formation stage of modern Saudi Arabia and Israel. Prior to the establishment of the Kingdom of Saudi Arabia in 1932, the Arabian Peninsula consisted of various tribes and regional powers. The Al Saud family, led by Abdulaziz Ibn Saud, gradually unified the disparate tribes through military conquests, forging alliances while proclaiming the establishment of the Kingdom of Saudi Arabia. Concurrently, the Zionist movement gained momentum in the late 19th and early 20th centuries, driven by the desire to establish a Jewish homeland in Palestine. Theodor Herzl, a key figure in the Zionist movement, proposed the idea of a Jewish state and pursued diplomatic efforts to secure international support.
2. Emergence of Saudi Arabia and Israel After the First World War, with the fall of the Ottoman Empire, the Middle East experienced significant changes. British and French influence shaped the region through the Sykes-Picot agreement, which partitioned the Arab territories. This arrangement, along with the Balfour Declaration of 1917 expressing British support for the establishment of a Jewish homeland in Palestine, laid the groundwork for the eventual formation of Saudi Arabia and Israel. However, tensions arose as Arab leaders and citizens viewed the establishment of a Jewish state as a betrayal, leading to widespread unrest and violent clashes.
3. Cold War Era Dynamics During the Cold War, the Middle

East became a battleground of influence between the United States and the Soviet Union. Saudi Arabia aligned itself with the United States, establishing a relationship based on strategic interests, especially regarding oil production and security. The United States sought to secure access to the vast oil reserves of the Arabian Peninsula and viewed Saudi Arabia as a key ally against Soviet influence. To maintain geopolitical stability, the U.S. provided military support and significant economic aid to Saudi Arabia. Israel, despite its socialist origins, also formed strong ties with the United States, largely driven by shared democratic values and mutual security concerns, particularly regarding the threat of Arab nationalism and Soviet influence in the region.

4. Arab-Israeli Conflicts The Arab-Israeli conflict, primarily centered around the Israeli-Palestinian dispute, has had a profound impact on regional dynamics and affected Saudi-Israeli relations. Saudi Arabia, as a leader among Arab nations, has consistently supported the Palestinian cause, advocating for a just resolution to the conflict and the establishment of a Palestinian state with East Jerusalem as its capital. This stance has often positioned Saudi Arabia opposite to Israel's policies, especially in relation to Israeli settlements in the West Bank and the status of Jerusalem. Arab states, including Saudi Arabia, participated in various military conflicts with Israel, such as the 1948 Arab-Israeli War, 1967 Six-Day War, and 1973 Yom Kippur War, exacerbating tensions between the two.

5. Regional Security Concerns Over time, Saudi Arabia and Israel began to find common ground on regional security issues. They shared concerns about Iran's regional influence, particularly due to its nuclear program and support for non-state actors such as Hezbollah in Lebanon and Hamas

in Palestine. Both countries also grapple with the threat of terrorism, with extremist groups targeting their respective territories and posing a significant security risk. This shared challenge has paved the way for limited cooperation and discreet contacts between intelligence agencies, as they exchange information and coordinate efforts to counter terrorism. Notably, intelligence collaboration intensified during the Obama administration, when Saudi Arabia and Israel, along with the United States, pursued covert operations against Iran's nuclear program through cyber attacks and sabotage.

6. Changing Regional Dynamics Recent years have witnessed a shifting regional landscape that has further shaped Saudi-Israeli relations. The rise of non-Arab regional powers, notably Iran and Turkey, has added complexities to the Middle Eastern geopolitical order. Saudi Arabia and Israel, recognizing the challenges posed by these emerging powers, have explored covert channels of communication and engaged in discreet cooperation to safeguard their shared interests. This has included intelligence sharing, clandestine meetings, and joint initiatives targeted at countering Iran's regional ambitions. Additionally, both nations have expressed concerns over the Arab Spring uprisings and subsequent turmoil, highlighting the need for stability and security within the region.

In conclusion, a deeper exploration of the historical context of Saudi-Israeli relations reveals a complex tapestry of alliances, conflicts, and shared challenges. From the pre-formation of modern states to the Arab-Israeli conflicts and evolving regional dynamics, these factors have influenced the trajectory of their interactions. Understanding this rich historical backdrop is critical for comprehending the intricate dynamics and potential future directions of Saudi-Israeli relations.

B. IMPORTANCE OF ANALYZING SAUDI-ISRAELI RELATIONS

Analyzing the relationship between Saudi Arabia and Israel holds immense importance in understanding the intricate dynamics of the Middle East and its impact on global politics. This chapter explores in-depth the key reasons why studying and comprehending this relationship is crucial for scholars, policymakers, and the general public.

Firstly, the significance of Saudi-Israeli relations lies in their potential to shape the broader Middle Eastern geopolitical landscape. Despite the absence of official diplomatic ties, these two countries, as influential actors in the region, exert considerable influence over regional conflicts, power dynamics, and political developments. By thoroughly examining their interactions, researchers can gain crucial insights into the complex web of alliances, rivalries, and power struggles that define the Middle East. Insights into how Saudi Arabia and Israel navigate these challenges, negotiate their regional interests, and maneuver within their respective spheres of influence are invaluable for understanding the broader geopolitical context and predicting future developments.

Secondly, the historical secrecy and ambiguity surrounding Saudi-Israeli relations make it all the more intriguing to explore. Both nations have traditionally maintained covert interactions, often operating through backchannel negotiations and discreet diplomatic maneuvers. Unraveling the underlying motivations and mechanisms employed by these two countries can uncover hidden strategies, clandestine collaborations, and the implications that shape Middle Eastern geopolitics. By studying this covert relationship, researchers can illuminate the nuances of their interactions, identify patterns and trends, and offer valuable insights into how these nations operate across various political landscapes.

Thirdly, Saudi-Israeli relations are crucial for addressing shared regional concerns. Both countries face common challenges, including Iranian influence in the region, the rise of extremist groups, and the pursuit of regional stability. A comprehensive analysis of their relationship allows us to better understand potential areas of collaboration, joint initiatives, and intelligence-sharing to address these shared threats. It helps policymakers assess the potential impact of their cooperation on broader regional dynamics and devise effective strategies to mitigate challenges.

Furthermore, examining Saudi-Israeli relations contributes to our comprehension of the influence of external actors on the Middle East. Powerful global players, such as the United States and other Western nations, have played vital roles in facilitating or hindering this relationship. By studying the motivations and actions of these external actors, we can gain a deeper understanding of the broader geopolitical chessboard and its impact on Saudi-Israeli interactions. This, in turn, helps policymakers and analysts gauge the influence of global powers on regional dynamics and anticipate potential shifts in alliances or strategies.

Moreover, analyzing Saudi-Israeli relations sheds light on the societal impact and domestic perspectives on this relationship. Both countries possess distinct religious identities, with Saudi Arabia being the epicenter of Islam and Israel being the Jewish homeland. The cultural and religious dimensions involved make their relationship a focal point for discussing the complexities of interfaith interactions in the Middle East. Exploring public opinion, cultural considerations, and the narratives perpetuated within these societies allows for a more nuanced understanding of the challenges and opportunities for closer ties. It also unveils societal barriers, religious sensitivities, and the diverse perspectives that shape public discourse, influencing the trajectory of bilateral relations.

In conclusion, the importance of analyzing Saudi-Israeli relations lies in the valuable insights it provides regarding the Middle East's political landscape, power dynamics, shared regional concerns, the role of external actors, and the cultural and religious dimensions involved. A comprehensive analysis facilitates a better understanding of international relations, informs policy decisions, and helps promote regional stability and peace. By studying this relationship, researchers, policymakers, and the general public can gain deeper insights into the Middle East's complex dynamics, contributing to a more informed and inclusive approach towards the region's challenges.

C. SCOPE AND PURPOSE OF THE BOOK

In order to fully grasp the complexities and significance of Saudi-Israeli relations, this chapter delves deeper into the scope and purpose of this book. By providing readers with a comprehensive understanding of what to expect, we aim to present a thorough exploration of the historical context, present relationships, and future prospects between these two nations.

The scope of this book extends beyond a mere surface-level analysis, as it aims to shed light on the multidimensional aspects that have shaped the Saudi-Israeli relationship. We recognize that

Saudi Arabia and Israel

this relationship is not static but rather dynamic and influenced by a myriad of interrelated factors. To comprehensively analyze and understand this complex relationship, we will adopt a multifaceted approach that encompasses political, economic, diplomatic, security, societal, and ethical dimensions.

To begin, we will delve into the historical scope of Saudi-Israeli relations, stretching back to their earliest interactions. By examining the historical context, readers will gain insights into the foundations of this relationship, including the impact of British colonial rule, Zionist aspirations, and the Arab nationalist movements throughout the first half of the 20th century. We will explore the key milestones, such as the establishment of the State of Israel in 1948, the 1967 Six-Day War, the 1973 Yom Kippur War, and subsequent peace agreements, to provide a comprehensive timeline of the evolving Saudi-Israeli relationship.

Furthermore, the book will analyze the present-day relationships between Saudi Arabia and Israel, taking into account the political and diplomatic engagements between the two nations. We will examine the post-Oslo Accords era, which witnessed semi-covert interactions between Saudi and Israeli officials, highlighting the intricate balancing acts faced by both countries. By analyzing official interactions, diplomatic initiatives, and strategic partnerships, readers will gain insights into the evolving nature of their relationship and the factors driving it. Additionally, we will explore covert aspects of their relationship, such as intelligence collaboration and unofficial channels of communication, to provide a comprehensive picture of their interactions and the complexities involved.

The economic dimension of Saudi-Israeli relations will also be explored in great detail. We recognize the significant impact that economic factors have on bilateral relations, including trade, investment, and economic cooperation. By analyzing the economic ties between Saudi Arabia and Israel, readers will gain an understanding of the opportunities and challenges that exist. We will explore areas of collaboration, such as technology exchange, joint ventures, and mutually beneficial economic projects that have the potential to foster stronger ties. Additionally, we will examine the energy dynamics between these nations, with a focus on the influence of oil and gas, as well as renewable energy cooperation.

Understanding the regional implications of the Saudi-Israeli relationship is crucial to comprehending the broader Middle Eastern dynamics. This book will analyze their roles in regional conflicts, such as the Arab-Israeli conflict and the Saudi-Iran rivalry. By examining their strategic calculations and policy alignments, readers will understand how the Saudi-Israeli relationship shapes the geopolitical landscape of the Middle East. We will explore the impact of their relationship on other regional actors, including Palestinian aspirations and Iranian influence, and discuss the prospects for broader Arab-Israeli normalization. Moreover, we will assess the implications of Saudi-Israeli cooperation on regional stability, its effect on the broader Arab world, and its relations with other key players such as the United States and Russia.

The societal impact and domestic perspectives on Saudi-Israeli relations will also be explored. We recognize that socio-cultural factors play a significant role in shaping international relations, and as such, we will examine public opinion, cultural, and religious implications, as well as societal reactions to the Saudi-Israeli relationship. By assessing the influence of religious beliefs, the Israel-Palestine conflict narrative, and governmental rhetoric on societal perceptions, readers will gain insight into the grassroots sentiment surrounding this relationship. Additionally, we will analyze the economic opportunities and challenges that arise from societal interactions, highlighting the potential for positive socio-economic developments as well as potential tensions.

Lastly, this book aims to address human rights concerns and

ethical dilemmas related to Saudi-Israeli relations. Given that both countries have faced criticism for their human rights records, it is imperative to explore this dimension of their relationship. By critically examining the human rights situations in Saudi Arabia and Israel, we will analyze the challenges of balancing strategic interests with fundamental humanitarian principles. This analysis will contribute to the ongoing discourse on the intersection of human rights and international relations, offering readers a comprehensive perspective on the ethical dimensions of the Saudi-Israeli relationship.

Overall, the purpose of this book is to provide readers with an in-depth understanding of the multifaceted Saudi-Israeli relationship. By examining the various dimensions of their relations, including the historical context, present relationships, economic interactions, regional implications, societal impact, and ethical considerations, readers will gain a deep appreciation for the significance and complexities of Saudi-Israeli relations. Through this comprehensive exploration, we hope to shed light on the opportunities, challenges, and future prospects that lie ahead for these two nations and their interaction on the global stage.

III

Historical Background

Throughout history, the interactions and relations between Saudi Arabia and Israel have been complex and shaped by various factors. Examining their historical background is essential to understanding the current dynamics between these two nations.

Early Interactions and Relations

Despite having no official diplomatic relations, Saudi Arabia and Israel have had limited interactions throughout history. During the early 20th century, the Zionist movement gained momentum, establishing a Jewish homeland in Palestine. This development sparked tensions with Arab nations, including Saudi Arabia.

Saudi Arabia, as a leader in the Arab world and custodian of the Islamic holy sites, played a significant role in opposing the establishment of a Jewish state.

King Abdulaziz Ibn Saud, the founder of modern Saudi Arabia, expressed solidarity with the Palestinians and rejected any recognition of Israel. He believed that the establishment of a Jewish state on Palestinian land would not only harm the Arab inhabitants but also threaten the sovereignty of Muslim holy sites in Jerusalem.

Despite this opposition, limited indirect engagements occurred between Saudi Arabia and Israel, primarily through diplomatic channels or discreet backchannel negotiations. In some cases, these discussions served as attempts to improve understanding, clarify positions, or explore potential avenues for collaboration.

Shifting Alliances during the Cold War

The Cold War period witnessed significant geopolitical realignments, influencing the Saudi-Israeli relationship. As an ally of the United States, Saudi Arabia aligned with Western powers, including Israel, against the Soviet Union and its influence in the Middle East.

While the Saudi leadership continued to adhere to its official stance of non-recognition, there were reports of secret meetings and intelligence sharing between Saudi Arabia and Israel during this time. These interactions aimed to enhance security cooperation, particularly regarding intelligence sharing, due to shared concerns over Soviet expansionism, pan-Arab nationalism, and the spread of communism.

However, due to the prevailing Arab sentiment against Israel, the Saudi leadership maintained a cautious approach in public. Officially, Saudi Arabia remained committed to the Palestinian cause and supported efforts to establish an independent Palestinian state.

The Arab-Israeli conflicts, particularly the 1948 war, the 1967 Six-Day War, and the 1973 Yom Kippur War, further strained relations between Saudi Arabia and Israel. Throughout these conflicts, Saudi Arabia provided significant financial and political support to Palestinian resistance movements, such as the Palestine Liberation

Organization (PLO). This support aimed to bolster the Palestinian cause and reclaim Palestinian territories occupied by Israel.

Shared Regional Concerns: Iran, Terrorism, and Stability

The rise of Iran as a regional power and the spread of Islamic extremism in the aftermath of the Iranian Revolution in 1979 shifted the dynamics of the Saudi-Israeli relationship. Both countries perceived Iran as a common threat due to its aggressive regional policies, support for militant groups, and nuclear ambitions.

These shared concerns prompted a gradual rapprochement between Saudi Arabia and Israel. While refraining from official recognition, the two nations engaged in discreet cooperation, particularly in intelligence sharing, security, and counterterrorism efforts. This cooperation aimed to counter Iran's influence and combat extremist organizations, such as Al-Qaeda and ISIS, which posed a direct threat to both countries.

Furthermore, the Israeli-Palestinian conflict also shaped Saudi-Israeli relations. As the Palestinian cause remained a central issue in the Arab world, Saudi Arabia sought to project itself as a key player in resolving the conflict. Under King Fahd bin Abdulaziz, the Saudi leadership proposed the Arab Peace Initiative in 2002, which aimed to achieve peace between Israel and the Arab states by offering normalization in exchange for a comprehensive resolution of the Israeli-Palestinian conflict.

Although Israel did not fully embrace this initiative, it signified Saudi Arabia's willingness to engage with Israel on a regional level and promote peace efforts. Subsequent Saudi monarchs, including King Abdullah bin Abdulaziz and King Salman bin Abdulaziz, supported peace initiatives and attempted to bridge the divide between Israel and Palestine through various diplomatic channels.

The Saudi-Israeli relationship has evolved further in recent years, partially driven by shared concerns over regional instability. The conflicts in Syria and Yemen, as well as the expansion of extremist groups like ISIS, have pushed both countries to explore potential areas of cooperation to mitigate these regional threats.

Understanding the historical context of Saudi-Israeli relations provides insights into the complex dynamics that continue to shape their current interactions. From initial opposition to limited cooperation and shared regional concerns, their relationship has undergone significant shifts influenced by geopolitical factors, regional conflicts, and efforts towards peace initiatives. This multifaceted history sets the stage for examining the present relationships between these two nations.

A. EARLY INTERACTIONS AND RELATIONS

Throughout history, the relationship between Saudi Arabia and Israel has been complex and shaped by a myriad of factors. This chapter delves into the early interactions and relations between the two countries, providing a foundation for understanding their current dynamics.

1.1 Pre-State Era and Secret Contacts

The earliest interactions between Saudi Arabia and Israel date back to the pre-state era of Israel when Jewish immigration to Palestine was increasing. While it was not publicly acknowledged, there were discreet contacts between certain Saudi leaders and prominent Zionists who were advocating for a Jewish homeland in Palestine.

These initial exchanges of ideas and exploratory discussions set the stage for future interactions between the two nations. These secret contacts were facilitated by individuals who believed that open communication and shared understanding could potentially alleviate tensions and resolve the conflict. Despite the prevailing anti-Zionist sentiment within much of the Arab world, these discreet conversations recognised that dialogue and engagement were necessary to address the region's complexities.

1.2 Post-1948 Period and Arab-Israeli Conflicts

Following the establishment of the State of Israel in 1948, Saudi Arabia, like most Arab countries, adopted a hostile stance towards Israel. The Arab-Israeli conflicts of the 20th century further strained relations between the two countries. Saudi Arabia, being a prominent Arab Muslim nation, aligned itself with the broader Arab consensus, supporting the Palestinians' quest for statehood and condemning Israel's occupation of Palestinian territories.

The Arab-Israeli conflicts shaped not only the regional political dynamics but also influenced the public opinion and consciousness within Saudi Arabia. The Israeli occupation of Jerusalem and the ongoing atrocities against Palestinians were viewed as injustices, resonating deeply with the population, which saw itself as the custodian of Islam's holiest sites in Mecca and Medina. The plight of the Palestinians became a rallying point for unity and resistance against what was perceived as Israeli aggression.

1.3 Behind-the-Scenes Interactions and Shared Concerns

Despite the public animosity, there were instances of behind-the-scenes interactions between Saudi Arabia and Israel. Shared concerns over regional stability and resistance against communism during the Cold War era primarily drove these interactions.

Intelligence sharing and discreet cooperation took place, although not openly acknowledged by the leadership of either country.

The fear of communism and its potential spread within the region prompted Saudi Arabia to engage in pragmatic relationships with other nations, including Israel. Both countries recognized the importance of countering common threats and safeguarding regional stability. While these interactions were shrouded in secrecy, they exemplified a willingness on the part of Saudi Arabia and Israel to put their differences aside in pursuit of shared goals.

1.4 Societal Attitudes and Religious/Cultural Factors

Societal attitudes towards Israel within Saudi Arabia were strongly influenced by religious and cultural factors. The Israeli occupation of Jerusalem and the ongoing conflict with the Palestinians held deep significance for Muslims, and Saudi Arabia, as the birthplace of Islam, played an influential role in shaping public opinion in the Arab and Muslim world. The Israeli-Palestinian conflict was viewed as an embodiment of the struggle for justice and self-determination for Palestinians.

The religious and cultural dimensions added complexity to the Saudi-Israeli relationship. The custodianship of Islam's holiest sites bestowed a sense of responsibility on the Saudi leaders to support the Palestinian cause and advocate for the liberation of Jerusalem. This deep-seated sentiment resonated with the broader population, which considered the occupation as a direct assault on their religion and cultural heritage.

However, it is important to note that pro-Israel sentiment emerged among some segments of the Saudi population, particularly those advocating for a more pragmatic approach to regional stability and recognizing the potential benefits of open engagement with Israel. These individuals believed in the possibility of mutual cooperation and economic prosperity through peaceful relations with Israel.

1.5 Dynamic Regional Context

The early interactions and relations between Saudi Arabia and Israel occurred in a region grappling with the aftermath of colonialism, the formation of new states, and multiple conflicts. Arab nationalism, pan-Arabism, and the pursuit of Palestinian self-determination were dominant forces shaping the collective Arab stance towards Israel.

Meanwhile, neighboring countries, such as Egypt and Jordan, established formal peace agreements with Israel, challenging the status quo and introducing new dynamics into the region. The evolving regional landscape influenced Saudi Arabia's approach to Israel as the country navigated its role as a regional power and protector of Islam's holiest sites.

The geopolitical landscape that emerged following the decolonization era prompted Saudi Arabia to reevaluate its relationship with Israel. Some Arab countries' recognition of Israel, formalized through peace agreements, and the shifting balance of power necessitated a reassessment of Saudi Arabia's stance. The country found itself at a crossroads, torn between the weight of historical Arab solidarity and the emerging realities of the region.

1.6 Conclusion

The early interactions and relations between Saudi Arabia and Israel laid the foundation for the complexities that exist in their relationship today. While public perceptions and official stances may have been marked by hostility, discreet interactions, shared concerns, and emerging pro-engagement sentiment among some within Saudi society have contributed to the nuanced nature of their relationship. Understanding these historical contexts provides valuable insights into the ongoing dynamics and potential for future developments between these two significant Middle Eastern nations.

B. SHIFTING ALLIANCES DURING THE COLD WAR

During the Cold War, the political dynamics in the Middle East underwent significant changes, particularly with regard to the alliances and relationships between Saudi Arabia and Israel. As the world was divided into two ideological camps, the United States-led Western bloc and the Soviet Union-led Eastern bloc, countries in the Middle East were often forced to align themselves with one side or the other.

In the early stages of the Cold War, Saudi Arabia maintained a distance from both the Eastern and Western blocs, prioritizing its own regional interests above ideological considerations. This approach was driven by the country's desire to ensure stability and security within its borders while safeguarding its oil resources, which were critical to its economic prosperity and global standing. Saudi Arabia's leadership also sought to balance its relationships with neighboring countries and maintain a prominent and independent role in the region's affairs.

However, as tensions increased in the region, the Saudi leadership gradually shifted towards the Western camp, aligning itself with the United States and its allies. This shift was partly driven by growing concerns over the expansionist ambitions of Soviet-backed regimes, such as Nasser's Egypt and the rise of pan-Arab nationalism. Saudi Arabia, as a conservative monarchy, saw these ideologies as a threat to its own stability and sought the protection of the United States against what it perceived as aggressive forces in the region.

Israel, on the other hand, emerged as a key ally of the United States in the Middle East during the Cold War. The creation of the state of Israel in 1948 and its subsequent independence marked a turning point in the region's geopolitics. The United States saw Israel as a strategic ally in countering Soviet influence in the region, and the two nations developed close military and intelligence cooperation during this period.

Saudi Arabia's initial reluctance to fully engage with Israel can be attributed, in part, to the country's emphasis on Arab solidarity and the Palestinian cause. Like many Arab countries, the Saudis staunchly supported the Palestinian struggle for self-determination and called for the establishment of a Palestinian state. As custodian of the holy sites of Islam, Saudi Arabia also faced domestic pressure to support Palestine and protect the status of Jerusalem, a city of immense religious significance to Muslims worldwide.

However, behind the scenes, there were indications of a covert engagement between Saudi Arabia and Israel during the Cold War. Despite the public stance against Israel, intelligence sharing and discreet diplomatic channels were established, as both countries recognized the need for cooperation to counter shared threats in the region. The Soviet Union's support for socialist and revolutionary movements in the Middle East further fueled their covert alignment.

Some argue that the Iranian Revolution in 1979 and the subsequent rise of extremist ideologies in the region further solidified the interests of Saudi Arabia and Israel. Both countries were alarmed by the growing influence of Iran and its support for proxy groups such as Hezbollah, which posed a threat to their respective security. The revolution transformed Iran into a bastion of anti-Western

Saudi Arabia and Israel

sentiment, causing concern for Saudi Arabia, while Israel viewed it as a regional adversary due to its support for Palestinian militant groups like Hamas.

These shifting alliances during the Cold War significantly shaped the subsequent dynamics between Saudi Arabia and Israel. While overt diplomatic relations were not established at that time, the foundations for future cooperation were laid, and both countries recognized the importance of maintaining discreet contact to protect their shared interests.

As the Cold War ended, the Middle East's geopolitical landscape continued to evolve. The fall of the Soviet Union and the dissolution of the Eastern bloc led to a recalibration of power dynamics, allowing for new possibilities and relationships to emerge. This historic context set the stage for further developments in Saudi-Israeli relations, with opportunities arising for deeper engagement and cooperation in the face of emerging challenges in the region.

In the post-Cold War period, the changing dynamics in the Middle East and the ongoing conflicts and regional rivalries created new geopolitical pressures for Saudi Arabia and Israel. Both countries found themselves increasingly isolated from their traditional allies, with the United States seeking to distance itself from Middle Eastern entanglements and other Arab nations growing skeptical of Saudi Arabia's leadership.

The Gulf War in the early 1990s was a turning point that further highlighted the shared interests between Saudi Arabia and Israel. The Iraqi invasion of Kuwait led to a massive international coalition, including both Saudi Arabia and Israel, forming against Saddam Hussein's aggression. While their cooperation remained limited and mainly focused on intelligence sharing and military coordination, it represented a significant step toward establishing a more visible partnership.

In the following years, the Oslo Accords between Israel and the

Palestine Liberation Organization (PLO) in the mid-1990s paved the way for a new era of regional possibilities. Saudi Arabia, along with other Arab countries, expressed their support for the peace process and held secret talks with Israeli officials to explore the potential for broader Arab-Israeli normalization. Although not leading to immediate diplomatic recognition, these engagements showcased a gradual convergence of interests between the Saudi leadership and Israel.

As the 21st century progressed, the rise of non-state actors, particularly extremist groups such as Al-Qaeda and later ISIS, reshaped the security landscape in the region. Saudi Arabia and Israel found themselves on the same side in the fight against terrorism, with a shared commitment to combating these common threats. Intelligence sharing, counter-terrorism cooperation, and discreet collaborative efforts became more pronounced behind the scenes, highlighting the deepening alignment between the two countries.

The changing dynamics in regional politics, the perceived threat from Iran's nuclear program, and the rise of a potential Iranian hegemony in the Middle East further catalyzed the Saudi-Israeli relationship. Although still primarily conducted away from media scrutiny, Saudi officials began openly discussing the possibility of cooperation with Israel on security matters. Statements by high-ranking Saudi officials, including Crown Prince Mohammed bin Salman, indicated a shift in Saudi Arabia's approach towards Israel.

This shifting landscape has led to some significant milestones in Saudi-Israeli relations in recent years. The Abraham Accords of 2020, which normalized diplomatic relations between Israel and several Arab countries, demonstrated a growing acceptance of Israel's presence in the region. Although Saudi Arabia did not explicitly join these accords, there has been speculation about the kingdom's potential future engagement.

The evolving Saudi-Israeli relationship, forged through discreet cooperation during the Cold War, has become increasingly visible and influential. While significant obstacles and sensitivities remain, the strategic convergence of interests, shared concerns, and the changing regional dynamics have laid the groundwork for a potential rapprochement between these former adversaries.

The relationship between Saudi Arabia and Israel will continue to be influenced by a complex web of geopolitical considerations, regional dynamics, and domestic factors. The evolving nature of Middle Eastern politics and the emergence of new challenges will require both countries to navigate a delicate balance between their interests, historical baggage, and regional expectations. As the winds of change blow through the Middle East, the story of Saudi-Israeli relations will undoubtedly continue to unfold, shaped by the intricate interplay of history, politics, and the pursuit of stability and security in an ever-changing region.

C. SHARED REGIONAL CONCERNS: IRAN, TERRORISM, AND STABILITY

The complex dynamics between Saudi Arabia and Israel are further shaped by their shared regional concerns regarding Iran, terrorism, and stability. Delving deeper into these concerns reveals the multifaceted nature of their relationship and the challenges that have influenced their interactions.

1. Iran:
a. Iran's Pursuit of Nuclear Weapons:

Both Saudi Arabia and Israel view Iran's nuclear program as a critical threat to regional stability. The potential for Iran to acquire nuclear weapons not only poses a direct security risk but also has significant implications for the existing balance of power in the region. Israel, having a tumultuous history with Iran due to Tehran's repeated calls for its destruction, sees the acquisition of nuclear weapons as an existential threat. On the other hand, Saudi Arabia, already locked in a fierce regional rivalry with Iran, worries about the consequences of a nuclear-capable Iran on its own security and regional influence. Both nations have consistently advocated for strict monitoring and limitations on Iran's nuclear activities.

b. Iranian Regional Influence:

The expanding Iranian influence in the region is a shared concern for Saudi Arabia and Israel. Iran's support for various proxy groups has allowed it to extend its reach beyond its borders. Hezbollah, backed by Iran, has played a significant role in Lebanon, exerting influence and attempting to undermine stability. This has direct implications for Saudi Arabia, which views Hezbollah as a destabilizing force, especially due to its alleged involvement in Yemen as supporters of the Houthi rebels challenging the internationally recognized government. Israel, having engaged in conflicts with Hezbollah in Lebanon, considers the group a major security threat that directly impacts its national security. The shared concern regarding Iran's regional influence provides a potential basis for cooperation between Saudi Arabia and Israel in countering Tehran's reach.

2. Terrorism:

a. Countering Sunni Extremism:

Both Saudi Arabia and Israel have faced challenges posed by Sunni extremist groups like ISIS and Al-Qaeda. These organizations, driven by violent ideologies, have become a significant threat not only to each country's security but also to regional stability. Saudi Arabia, in particular, has recognized the need to address the roots of extremism within its own society and has implemented reforms to counter radical ideologies. Israel, too, has strengthened its intelligence and security measures to counter the risks posed by terrorist organizations. The Saudi-Israeli cooperation in countering Sunni extremism has been limited due to political sensitivities but holds the potential for further collaboration considering the shared threat.

b- Shia Militancy:

Saudi Arabia and Israel have also confronted challenges arising from Shia militant groups backed by Iran, such as Hezbollah. These groups have engaged in acts of terrorism and have further inflamed regional tensions. Saudi Arabia has faced direct experiences with Hezbollah's involvement in Lebanon and its alleged support for Houthi rebels in Yemen, disrupting its national security interests. Israel, engaged in intermittent conflicts with Hezbollah, perceives the group as a significant security concern. Both Saudi Arabia and Israel share a mutual concern over Shia militancy supported by Iran, leading to increased cooperation in countering Iranian influence and its proxy activities in the region.

3. Regional Stability:

a. Sectarian Divisions:

The long-standing Sunni-Shia divide poses a significant challenge to regional stability, and both Saudi Arabia and Israel share concerns regarding its implications. Sectarian tensions have fueled conflicts and created a hostile environment that threatens peace and security in the region. Saudi Arabia perceives itself as a leader of the Sunni world, and any rise in Shia influence challenges the existing power balance. Israel, as a predominantly Jewish state, faces difficulties in establishing diplomatic relationships with predominantly

Arab and Muslim countries due to sectarian sensitivities. Both countries are interested in mitigating sectarian divisions to promote regional peace and stability.

b. Spillover Effects:

The ongoing conflicts in Syria, Iraq, and Yemen have had profound spillover effects, posing significant threats to neighboring countries, including Saudi Arabia and Israel. Syria's civil war has resulted in a massive influx of refugees into neighboring countries, straining their resources and security apparatus. Additionally, the Syrian conflict has created a power vacuum that has allowed terrorist groups like ISIS to establish a foothold, posing direct threats to regional stability. In Yemen, the ongoing conflict between Houthi rebels supported by Iran and the internationally recognized government supported by a Saudi-led coalition has further highlighted the region's fragility. Both Saudi Arabia and Israel have felt the repercussions of these conflicts, leading to increased efforts to address the root causes and seek collective solutions.

The shared concerns regarding Iran, terrorism, and stability expose the intricacies of Saudi-Israeli relations and the potential for cooperation. While political considerations have limited the depth of collaboration, recognising common threats has driven them to explore opportunities for collective actions. By proactively addressing these shared concerns, Saudi Arabia and Israel can contribute to promoting stability, security, and prosperity in the Middle East.

IN A NUTSHELL

A. Early Interactions and Relations

The historical background of Saudi-Israeli relations begins with a foundational lack of formal diplomatic ties, largely due to Saudi Arabia's strong opposition to the establishment of Israel. In 1947, Saudi Arabia voted against the United Nations Partition Plan for Palestine, which aimed to create separate Jewish and Arab states in the region. This opposition was rooted in support for Palestinian Arabs and a broader Arab solidarity against the establishment of a Jewish state. Despite the absence of formal relations, there have been instances of covert cooperation between the two states, particularly when facing common enemies. For example, during the Yemen Civil War in the 1960s, both nations supported Yemeni royalists against the Egyptian-backed republicans, with Israel even allegedly allowing arms shipments to pass through its territory to assist the royalists.

B. Shifting Alliances during the Cold War

During the Cold War, the geopolitical landscape influenced shifts in alliances and interactions in the Middle East, including between Saudi Arabia and Israel. The United States' efforts to establish an anti-Soviet alliance system in the region often alienated both Israel and Arab nations, including Egypt and Saudi Arabia. However, the regional dynamics led to occasional covert cooperation between Saudi Arabia and Israel, particularly in contexts where both faced threats from common adversaries like radical Arab nationalism led by figures such as Egyptian President Gamal Abdel Nasser.

C. Shared Regional Concerns: Iran, Terrorism, and Stability

In more recent years, shared concerns over regional threats such as Iran's influence, terrorism, and the need for stability have brought Saudi Arabia and Israel into a closer, albeit still unofficial, alignment. Both countries view Iran as a significant security threat, particularly due to its nuclear ambitions, support for Hezbollah in Lebanon, and its role in conflicts across the region. This mutual concern has fostered a quiet revolution in Saudi-Israeli relations, with increased intelligence sharing and cooperation behind the scenes.

The threat of terrorism and the need for regional stability have also played roles in bringing the nations closer. Both Saudi Arabia and Israel are interested in countering extremist groups that destabilize the region. The rise of ISIS and other terrorist organizations has necessitated cooperation on security matters, not only between these two countries but also among broader regional and international partners.

Furthermore, the Abraham Accords of 2020, which saw the normalization of relations between Israel and several Arab states, including the UAE and Bahrain, have potentially set the stage for Saudi Arabia to follow suit. While Saudi Arabia has not yet formally normalized relations with Israel, the shifting regional alliances and the common interests in countering Iran's influence and promoting stability continue to push Saudi Arabia and Israel towards a pragmatic albeit cautious rapprochement.

In conclusion, the historical background of Saudi-Israel relations is marked by initial opposition and lack of formal ties, covert cooperation during periods of mutual threat, and a recent shift towards closer, if unofficial, relations driven by shared concerns over regional threats like Iran, terrorism, and the overarching need for stability.

Sources and References

[1] https://apps.dtic.mil/sti/trecms/pdf/AD1164221.pdf
[2] https://www.theguardian.com/world/2024/apr/19/gulf-states-response-to-iran-israel-conflict-may-decide-outcome-of-crisis
[3] https://russiancouncil.ru/en/blogs/a-khalfa/evolution-of-saudiisrael-relations-unveiling-the-shift-from-quiet-dipl/
[4] https://en.wikipedia.org/wiki/Israel%E2%80%93Saudi_Arabia_relations
[5] https://ip-quarterly.com/en/hamas-israel-and-cold-war-gulf
[6] https://www.brookings.edu/articles/how-to-understand-israel-and-saudi-arabias-secretive-relationship/
[7] https://www.cambridge.org/core/books/abs/cold-wars/arabisraeli-relations-194864/BED2E8EDDDCF11D9A538F5B6250F8C70
[8] https://www.atlantis-press.com/article/125961797.pdf
[9] https://pomeps.org/shifting-alliances-and-shifting-theories-in-the-middle-east
[10] https://digitalworks.union.edu/cgi/viewcontent.cgi?article=1698&context=theses
[11] https://academic.oup.com/book/36791/chapter-abstract/321938296?redirectedFrom=fulltext
[12] https://peacerep.org/2023/04/25/iran-regional-policy-israel/
[13] https://carnegieendowment.org/2023/10/13/arab-perspectives-on-middle-east-crisis-pub-90774
[14] https://press.un.org/en/2020/sc14333.doc.htm
[15] https://www.tandfonline.com/doi/full/10.1080/13537121.2023.2206209

[16] https://www.ispionline.it/en/publication/israel-iran-escalation-reactions-from-the-region-and-beyond-170441

[17] https://ecfr.eu/publication/proxy-battles-iraq-iran-and-the-turmoil-in-the-middle-east/

[18] https://hansard.parliament.uk/commons/2024-04-15/debates/5B1C3E28-F71B-4513-B1D8-54205AF8D464/Iran-IsraelUpdate

[19] https://www.cbc.ca/news/world/israel-iran-saudi-arabia-jordan-1.7176154

IV

Present Relationships

Saudi Arabia and Israel have maintained a complex and nuanced relationship in recent years, characterized by a combination of publicly acknowledged contacts and significant behind-the-scenes collaboration. While not officially recognized diplomatically, both countries have tried to engage with each other, particularly in addressing shared regional concerns.

Publicly Acknowledged Contacts and Diplomatic Developments

Over the past decade, there have been several instances of publicly acknowledged contacts between Saudi Arabia and Israel. These interactions have taken the form of diplomatic visits, official meetings, and even high-level summits. While initially met with skepticism and controversy, these developments indicate a willingness on both sides to engage in open dialogue and build a level of understanding.

Saudi Arabia and Israel

One significant example of such public contact was the historic visit of then-Crown Prince Muhammad bin Salman to Israel in 2018. Although the official purpose of the visit was to discuss regional security dynamics, this unprecedented event sent shockwaves throughout the Middle East and beyond. It signaled a potential shift in Saudi policy towards Israel and sparked debates regarding the future trajectory of their relationship.

Despite the lack of official diplomatic relations, Saudi Arabia has taken steps to publicly acknowledge Israel's existence and its right to security. In September 2020, the Kingdom allowed the use of its airspace for the first direct commercial flights between Israel and the United Arab Emirates (UAE), signaling a relaxation of long-standing travel restrictions and the willingness to openly engage with Israel. This move not only paved the way for enhanced economic and cultural ties but also set a precedent for other Arab countries in the region.

Furthermore, the Abraham Accords, signed in September 2020 between Israel, the UAE, and Bahrain, marked a significant diplomatic breakthrough in the region. While Saudi Arabia did not officially join the Accords, its support and behind-the-scenes involvement played a crucial role in their realization. This demonstrated the Kingdom's strategic alignment with Israel and its willingness to be a facilitator of regional peace efforts.

Behind-the-Scenes Cooperation: Intelligence Sharing and Defense

Behind closed doors, Saudi Arabia and Israel have been actively collaborating on intelligence sharing and defense matters. Both countries face similar security threats, particularly from Iran and non-state actors like Hezbollah and Hamas. The exchange of intelligence has enabled them to counter these threats and safeguard their respective interests effectively.

It is widely believed that Mossad, Israel's intelligence agency, and Saudi Arabia's General Intelligence Presidency (GIP) have established covert channels for information sharing. This collaboration has been instrumental in countering terrorism and uncovering regional destabilization activities.

Together, Saudi Arabia and Israel aim to counter Iran's aggressive ambitions in the region, with a particular focus on monitoring its nuclear program and preventing the spread of Iranian influence. The intelligence sharing and cooperation extend to thwarting terrorist financing networks and sharing expertise in cyber defense, further reinforcing the strategic partnership between the two countries.

In addition to intelligence sharing, there have been reports of defense collaborations between Saudi Arabia and Israel, including the acquisition of advanced military technology and joint military training exercises. While the specifics are often kept confidential, these collaborations demonstrate the depth of their security cooperation and the recognition of each other's capabilities in addressing common threats.

Economic Collaborations and Trade Agreements

In recent years, economic collaborations and trade agreements have also played a role in Saudi-Israeli relations. Amidst Saudi Arabia's efforts to diversify its economy through its Vision 2030 initiative, there has been a growing interest in developing economic ties with Israel, known for its technological advancements and innovation.

While the public acknowledgement of economic interactions remains limited, reports suggest that the two countries have increased engagement in trade and investment activities. These interactions are channelled through intermediaries and third-party entities to maintain a level of deniability, given the sensitive nature of their relationship.

One such example of economic collaboration is the potential partnership between Saudi Arabia's Public Investment Fund (PIF) and Israeli technology companies. The PIF, under Vision 2030, aims to invest in innovative ventures and diversify the Saudi economy. Israeli businesses, known for their technological prowess, can offer valuable expertise and opportunities for joint ventures in artificial intelligence, cybersecurity, healthcare, and renewable energy sectors.

Moreover, discussions have been on leveraging Israeli technological advancements in the agricultural sector to address Saudi Arabia's food security challenges. Israeli expertise in water management and desert agriculture has the potential to enhance Saudi Arabia's agricultural productivity and sustainability, contributing to the achievement of the Kingdom's Vision 2030 goals.

By fostering economic collaborations, Saudi Arabia and Israel not only reap the benefits of technological advancements but also build interdependencies, fostering stability and cooperation in the region. The economic integration between the two countries can serve as a catalyst for a broader Arab-Israeli rapprochement, transforming regional dynamics and promoting a more prosperous future.

Overall, the present relationships between Saudi Arabia and Israel are characterized by a delicate balance of public acknowledgement and behind-the-scenes collaboration. While diplomatic recognition is yet to be established, the growing engagements in various spheres demonstrate a recognition of shared interests and potential for future cooperation. These relationships can potentially shape the dynamics of the Middle East and have significant implications for regional stability and global diplomacy.

A. PUBLICLY ACKNOWLEDGED CONTACTS AND DIPLOMATIC DEVELOPMENTS

In recent years, a notable shift has taken place in the historically elusive relationship between Saudi Arabia and Israel. This section explores the publicly acknowledged contacts and diplomatic developments between these two nations, analyzing their implications for the countries involved and the broader Middle East region. It explores the motivations driving these engagements, the reactions they have elicited, and the potential impact they may have on future Saudi Arabia-Israel relations.

The Visit of Crown Prince Mohammed bin Salman to Israel (2018):

One of the watershed moments in the evolving Saudi-Israeli relationship was the low-key visit of Saudi Crown Prince Mohammed bin Salman to Israel in 2018. Although not widely publicized, the international community took notice. This unorthodox visit clearly signals Saudi Arabia's willingness to engage with Israel on a more public level, breaking from the longstanding tradition of secrecy and ambiguity.

The visit coincided with broader regional shifts, including the changing perception of the Israeli-Palestinian conflict among some

Arab states. It symbolized a desire to move beyond the traditional enmity towards Israel and explore avenues for cooperation. However, deep-rooted sensitivities surrounding the Palestinian cause and the lack of progress in the peace process continue to pose challenges to the depth of this evolving relationship.

Ongoing Diplomatic Encounters:

In addition to Crown Prince Mohammed bin Salman's visit, there have been further instances of diplomatic encounters between Saudi Arabia and Israel. High-level meetings and consultations have taken place, allowing officials from both sides to discuss regional challenges and explore potential areas of cooperation.

These diplomatic engagements encompass various dimensions, including security coordination, intelligence sharing, economic partnerships, and technological collaborations. Discussions have focused on countering Iran's destabilizing activities, combating terrorism, and addressing common security concerns. Furthermore, economic exchanges have gained momentum, with discussions revolving around investments, trade, and tourism. These developments highlight the potential benefits and shared interests that underpin these diplomatic encounters.

Public Discourse and Dialogue:

Another significant aspect of the shifting Saudi-Israeli relationship is the rise of public discourse and dialogue between figures from both countries. Op-eds in major newspapers and interviews with leaders have allowed them to express their perspectives on regional matters, highlighting potential areas of cooperation and shared interests.

Prominent Saudi and Israeli voices have emphasized the need

for a pragmatic approach to regional challenges, transcending past hostilities. Mutual recognition of the importance of stability and prosperity in the Middle East has driven public discussions on energy cooperation, water resource management, and technology transfer. These public exchanges have enabled Saudi Arabia and Israel to test public sentiment and helped shape narratives that pave the way for future diplomatic initiatives.

The Complex Nature of the Relationship:

While the aforementioned developments mark a notable shift, it is essential to recognize the complexities inherent in the Saudi-Israeli relationship. The historical Arab consensus on the Palestinian-Israeli conflict, coupled with Saudi Arabia's commitment to the Arab Peace Initiative, imposes limitations on the extent of engagement with Israel.

The Palestinian-Israeli conflict remains a deeply complex and sensitive issue, with long-standing implications for Arab-Israeli relations. Publicly acknowledging contacts and diplomatic engagements with Israel does not imply the establishment of formal diplomatic relations between Saudi Arabia and Israel or the abandonment of shared Arab narratives. It is essential to foster an understanding that any future developments will likely be contingent upon significant progress in the Israeli-Palestinian peace process.

Conclusion:

The publicly acknowledged contacts and diplomatic developments between Saudi Arabia and Israel are indicative of a gradual but significant shift in their relationship. The motivations driving these engagements, including shared regional concerns and the recognition of mutual interests, suggest the potential for increased cooperation in the future. However, it is vital to exercise caution and acknowledge the complexities inherent in the Saudi-Israeli relationship, particularly with regard to the Palestinian-Israeli conflict. The ongoing dialogue and engagement between these nations provide a promising foundation for potential future developments but should be tempered with a balanced and nuanced approach that considers regional dynamics, aspirations for peace, and the preservation of the Arab consensus.

B. BEHIND-THE-SCENES COOPERATION: INTELLIGENCE SHARING AND DEFENSE

This section explores the less-publicized aspects of Saudi-Israeli relations, focusing specifically on intelligence sharing, defense collaborations, and the broader implications of their behind-the-scenes cooperation. While overt diplomatic relations between Saudi Arabia and Israel may still be limited, there is growing evidence pointing to a significant degree of covert cooperation in the realms of intelligence, defense, and beyond. This chapter uncovers the intricacies of this cooperation and explores its implications for regional dynamics, alliances, and the prospects for peace in the Middle East.

Espionage and Security Cooperation:

Intelligence Exchange:
Despite their historical differences, Saudi Arabia and Israel have found common ground in their shared security concerns. Both

countries face threats from regional adversaries, such as Iran and its proxies, as well as the rise of extremist ideologies. These mutual interests have driven intelligence agencies in the two states to establish discreet channels for information sharing, counterterrorism efforts, and monitoring of regional developments.

Behind closed doors, intelligence agencies in Saudi Arabia and Israel have cultivated robust relationships built on trust and reliability. Classified information, including assessments of regional threats, surveillance data, and analysis of political and military developments, is exchanged on a regular basis between the agencies. These intelligence exchanges contribute to a more accurate understanding of the regional landscape and aid in formulating effective strategies to counter common adversaries.

Joint Operations:

In addition to intelligence sharing, Saudi and Israeli intelligence agencies have reportedly engaged in joint operations to combat terrorism, disrupt extremist networks, and gather intelligence on common adversaries. These covert collaboration efforts have proven highly effective in mitigating security threats and maintaining regional stability.

Under the framework of these joint operations, intelligence agents from both countries work together to analyze, track, and apprehend individuals suspected of involvement in extremist activities. By pooling their resources and expertise, Saudi and Israeli intelligence agencies have succeeded in foiling numerous terrorist plots that could have had far-reaching consequences for the region. These joint operations reflect a level of cooperation and coordination unprecedented in the history of Saudi-Israeli relations.

Cybersecurity Collaboration:

Alongside traditional intelligence sharing, Saudi Arabia and Israel have expanded their cooperation to include cybersecurity. With the increasing prominence of cyber threats, both countries have recognized the importance of sharing information, best practices, and technology to counter cyber espionage, attacks, and protect critical infrastructure.

Collaboration in the field of cybersecurity has been instrumental in improving the cyber defenses of both Saudi Arabia and Israel. Through joint efforts, they exchange expertise in detecting advanced persistent threats, analyzing malware, and implementing cutting-edge technologies to enhance their cyber resilience. This collaboration extends beyond bilateral cooperation, as both countries share information with other regional partners facing similar cyber challenges. This collective approach bolsters the cybersecurity posture of the entire region.

Shared Interests in Regional Stability:

Concerns over Iran:

Saudi Arabia and Israel both view the Iranian regime as a significant threat to regional stability. Their shared opposition to Iran's regional ambitions, involvement in proxy conflicts, and pursuit of nuclear capabilities have provided a strong impetus for clandestine cooperation. Intelligence sharing and joint efforts aim to monitor Iranian activities, counter its influence, and plan for potential contingencies.

Within the realm of intelligence sharing, Saudi Arabia and Israel exchange critical information on Iran's nuclear program, ballistic missile development, and regional activities. This knowledge helps both countries assess the potential security implications and develop proactive measures to address Iran's threats. Additionally, joint analysis of Iran's support for militant groups and its infiltration into neighboring countries allows Saudi Arabia and Israel to respond effectively, both independently and collectively.

Counteracting Extremism:
Extremist ideologies have plagued the Middle East, and Saudi Arabia and Israel share a common interest in combatting these forces. The exchange of information on extremist organizations, radicalization networks, and financing mechanisms has played a crucial role in identifying and neutralizing threats to their respective countries and the broader region.

Saudi Arabia and Israel's cooperation in countering extremism extends beyond intelligence sharing. Both countries have leveraged their experiences and resources to develop comprehensive strategies for countering radicalization and extremist propaganda. This includes joint initiatives to monitor online activities, intercept illicit financial flows, and share best practices in preventive measures. Such collaborative efforts have proven instrumental in disrupting the recruitment and radicalization process, reducing extremist organisations' influence, and enhancing both nations' security.

Military and Defense Cooperation:
In addition to intelligence sharing and counterterrorism efforts, Saudi Arabia and Israel have quietly expanded their military and defense collaborations. While specific details are often kept under wraps due to the topic's sensitivity, mounting evidence suggests joint military exercises, technology transfers, and intelligence-driven operations.

These defense collaborations have allowed both countries to enhance their military capabilities, streamline their defense industries, and strengthen their deterrence against common adversaries. Shared expertise in missile defense systems, aerial surveillance,

Saudi Arabia and Israel

and special operations allows Saudi Arabia and Israel to leverage their comparative advantages and bolster their defenses in an ever-evolving regional security landscape.

Implications for Broader Middle Eastern Dynamics:

Impact on Regional Alliances:

The covert cooperation between Saudi Arabia and Israel has potential ramifications for the established alliances in the Middle East. Traditional alliances among Arab states, shaped by historical enmity towards Israel, may undergo a transformation as shared security concerns open doors for closer cooperation between traditional adversaries. This shift could reconfigure power dynamics in the region.

The discreet cooperation between Saudi Arabia and Israel challenges historical notions of enmity and serves as a catalyst for potential realignments in regional alliances. The shared security interests between these two countries have already fostered a degree of collaboration with certain Gulf states, namely the United Arab Emirates and Bahrain, who have recently normalized relations with Israel. This convergence of interests may further extend to other Arab countries seeking to mitigate common threats and benefit from the expertise exchange and technological prowess of both Saudi Arabia and Israel.

Effects on Peace Process:

The clandestine collaboration between Saudi Arabia and Israel affects the prospects for a lasting resolution to the Israeli-Palestinian conflict. While Saudi Arabia has long supported the Arab Peace

Initiative, which envisions full normalization of relations with Israel in exchange for a comprehensive peace agreement, covert cooperation may complicate the delicate balance within the Arab world regarding Israel.

The behind-the-scenes cooperation between Saudi Arabia and Israel introduces a complex dynamic to the Israeli-Palestinian conflict. While Saudi Arabia publicly advocates for a two-state solution and the establishment of a Palestinian state, their growing covert cooperation with Israel may draw criticism from other Arab states and Palestine. The delicate balancing act faced by Saudi Arabia necessitates discreet cooperation with Israel while maintaining credibility within the Arab world and before its own citizens, who overwhelmingly support the Palestinian cause.

Broader Dynamics in the Middle East:

The growing clandestine ties between Saudi Arabia and Israel could have broader implications for the political landscape across the Middle East. The alignment of interests between the two countries may impact regional conflicts, alliances, and power balances, presenting both opportunities and challenges for stabilizing the region.

As intelligence sharing, defense collaborations, and other forms of cooperation between Saudi Arabia and Israel expand, they have the potential to reshape regional dynamics. The convergence of interests in countering Iran, combating extremism, and ensuring stability serves as a catalyst for cooperation beyond traditional adversaries. This evolving clandestine relationship could act as a stabilizing force in a region haunted byinstability, creating new avenues for dialogue, and potentially reducing tensions between key regional players.

The growing cooperation between Saudi Arabia and Israel signals a shift in the Middle Eastern landscape, with shared security concerns outweighing historical animosities. This evolving relationship challenges conventional wisdom and opens up possibilities for new regional alliances that transcend religious and political differences. It also presents an opportunity to address common challenges that have plagued the Middle East for decades, fostering stability and prosperity.

However, this cooperation's covert nature poses its own challenges. The sensitivity surrounding the relationship necessitates careful management to maintain the delicate balance between collaboration with Israel and maintaining credibility within the Arab world. Saudi Arabia must navigate the complexities of its regional relationships and the Israeli-Palestinian conflict to ensure its covert cooperation with Israel does not undermine its standing or jeopardize its aspirations for a comprehensive peace agreement.

Furthermore, the growing cooperation between Saudi Arabia and Israel could also face resistance from other states in the region. Traditional alliances, such as the Arab League, have historically supported the Palestinian cause and have been critical of Israeli actions. The progress made in covert cooperation between Saudi Arabia and Israel may not be universally welcomed, particularly by states that have been reluctant to normalize relations with Israel.

Overall, the behind-the-scenes cooperation between Saudi Arabia and Israel in the realms of intelligence sharing, defense collaborations, and beyond has significant implications for the broader dynamics of the Middle East. While it presents opportunities for countering shared threats, enhancing regional stability, and potentially paving the way for new alliances, it also poses challenges in terms of managing regional sensitivities and the complexities of the Israeli-Palestinian conflict. The true extent and impact of this cooperation will require continued observation and analysis as the Middle East continues to evolve.

C. ECONOMIC COLLABORATIONS AND TRADE AGREEMENTS

Economic collaborations and trade agreements have become pivotal in the steadily evolving Saudi-Israeli relationship. Over the years, the economic ties between the two countries have expanded beyond their historical limitations, with recent developments showcasing a remarkable increase in trade and investment activities. This extended chapter will delve deeper into the economic collaborations and trade agreements between Saudi Arabia and Israel, shedding light on their broader impact on both nations and the overall regional dynamics.

The Saudi-Israeli economic relationship has significantly transformed, driven by a strategic realignment of interests, geopolitical shifts, and shared regional challenges. Both countries recognize the urgent need to diversify their economies and attract foreign investments, leading them to explore economic opportunities and forge collaborations. From agriculture to technology, numerous sectors have emerged as focal points for cooperation, intertwining the mutual interests of both nations.

In agriculture, Israel's expertise in advanced agricultural technologies has proved invaluable to Saudi Arabia, which grapples with similar challenges due to its arid climate. Through knowledge sharing and technology transfer, Saudi Arabia has sought to enhance its food production capabilities and optimize water management practices, addressing the increasing demands for food security and environmental sustainability. The exchange of innovative farming techniques and the development of new technologies, facilitated by joint research and development programs between Saudi Arabian and Israeli institutions, hold the potential to revolutionize agricultural practices in both nations.

Furthermore, the steady growth of trade agreements and partnerships has fostered economic exchanges between Saudi Arabia and Israel. While formal trade relations between the two nations still face notable barriers, indirect trade has experienced a significant surge facilitated by intermediary countries. These trade routes not only enable both countries to bypass formal restrictions but also contribute to the expansion of bilateral trade volumes, laying the foundation for further economic integration.

The recent normalization of diplomatic relations between Saudi Arabia and Israel has created new opportunities for economic collaboration. The establishment of direct commercial flights between the two nations has not only simplified logistics but has also bolstered trade and tourism. This remarkable development has fostered cultural exchanges and deepened mutual understanding, ultimately facilitating the growth of business ties, which, in turn, drive economic cooperation.

Investment cooperation between Saudi Arabia and Israel has gained considerable momentum, with both nations recognizing the significant potential for economic growth and collaboration. Saudi Arabia's Public Investment Fund has shown a keen interest in investing in Israeli innovation and technology, with specific emphasis on sectors such as renewable energy, infrastructure development, and healthcare. This investment approach aims to capitalize on Israel's renowned startup ecosystem and technological advancements, fostering knowledge sharing, research collaborations, and mutual economic benefits.

The economic collaborations and trade agreements between Saudi Arabia and Israel hold considerable regional significance.

These developments contribute to shifting regional dynamics and have the potential to unlock new avenues for cooperation across various fields. The shared interest in economic development has provided a stepping stone for greater understanding and cooperation, presenting an opportunity to bridge historical divides and promote peace in the region.

However, it is essential to acknowledge that despite the progress made, challenges continue to exist in fully harnessing the economic potential of the Saudi-Israeli relationship. Political sensitivities, historical animosities, and ongoing regional conflicts still pose significant obstacles to further deepening economic collaborations. Overcoming these challenges requires sustained efforts and diplomatic initiatives to build trust and address the underlying issues. Nevertheless, the commitment of both nations to realizing the mutual benefits of increased economic engagement remains steadfast.

In conclusion, Saudi Arabia and Israel's economic collaborations and trade agreements have witnessed notable growth in recent years. Recognizing the shared opportunities and benefits, both nations have embarked on economic integration and diversification. These collaborations not only enhance bilateral trade and investment but also have the potential to contribute to regional stability and prosperity. Continued efforts to strengthen economic ties will create a more interconnected and economically integrated Middle East, fostering a positive ripple effect throughout the region. The evolving economic relationship between Saudi Arabia and Israel represents a significant milestone in the region's history, paving the way for a future built on shared economic interests and cooperation.

IN A NUTSHELL

A. Publicly Acknowledged Contacts and Diplomatic Developments

Saudi Arabia and Israel have had a series of publicly acknowledged contacts and diplomatic developments, particularly in light of the shifting dynamics in the Middle East. Saudi Arabia's Foreign Minister stated in January 2024 that the kingdom could recognize Israel if a comprehensive agreement were reached that included statehood for the Palestinians. This statement reflects a potential shift in Saudi policy, contingent upon the resolution of the Palestinian issue.

In September 2023, Israeli Prime Minister Benjamin Netanyahu expressed confidence in a "historic" US-brokered agreement to establish formal diplomatic relations with Saudi Arabia during talks with US President Joe Biden. This indicates a growing public acknowledgment of the possibility of normalization between the two countries.

Moreover, Saudi Arabia has publicly acknowledged its involvement in aiding the newly formed regional military coalition in defending Israel against an Iranian attack. This acknowledgment came in the form of a summary on its official website, citing insights from a source within the Saudi royal family.

B. Behind-the-Scenes Cooperation: Intelligence Sharing and Defense

Behind-the-scenes cooperation between Saudi Arabia and

Israel, particularly in intelligence sharing and defense, has become more frequent and routine. Multiple Gulf States, including Saudi Arabia, shared intelligence about Iran's plans to attack Israel, which significantly contributed to the successful implementation of air defense measures. This cooperation was spearheaded by the US and involved an informal military alliance aimed at countering threats from Iran.

In April 2024, an unprecedented attack by Iran on Israel was largely thwarted due to the multilayered air defense network of Israel, bolstered by the US and its allies, with approximately 99% of the incoming threats neutralized. The success of this defense effort was attributed to the intelligence sharing and active participation in intercepting threats by countries like Saudi Arabia, which do not maintain diplomatic ties with Israel.

C. Economic Collaborations and Trade Agreements

Economic relations between Israel and the Gulf States, including Saudi Arabia, have been developing, albeit without official diplomatic and trade relations. Reports indicate that Affinity Partners, Jared Kushner's private equity fund, is planning to invest money from the sovereign wealth fund of Saudi Arabia in Israeli enterprises. This suggests a growing interest in economic collaboration despite the lack of formal ties.

The UAE-Israel Comprehensive Economic Partnership Agreement (CEPA) is an example of the increasing economic collaborations in the region. The agreement, which came into force in April 2023, provides greater market access across multiple sectors for both trade in goods and services, with over 96% of tariffs removed or reduced immediately. While Saudi Arabia is not a signatory to this agreement, the trend of increasing economic ties between Israel and Gulf States could potentially influence future Saudi-Israeli economic collaborations.

In summary, Saudi Arabia and Israel's relationship has evolved to include publicly acknowledged contacts, behind-the-scenes cooperation in intelligence sharing and defense, and potential economic collaborations. These developments reflect a pragmatic approach by both countries in addressing shared regional concerns, despite the absence of formal diplomatic relations.

Sources and References

[1] https://www.i24news.tv/en/news/middle-east/artc-saudi-arabia-publicly-acknowledges-role-in-defending-israel-against-iranian-attack
[2] https://manaramagazine.org/2022/07/economic-relations-between-israel-and-the-gulf-states/
[3] https://www.brookings.edu/articles/how-to-understand-israel-and-saudi-arabias-secretive-relationship/
[4] https://abc7chicago.com/drones-and-missiles-iran-launched-intercepted-israel-attack-middle-east-why-is-attacking/14662141/
[5] https://www.aljazeera.com/news/2023/9/20/israel-saudi-arabia-normalisation-deal-in-reach-netanyahu-tells-biden
[6] https://en.wikipedia.org/wiki/Israel%E2%80%93Saudi_Arabia_relations
[7] https://www.atlanticcouncil.org/blogs/menasource/saudi-arabia-israel-two-state-gaza-normalization/
[8] https://www.timesofisrael.com/report-gulf-states-including-saudi-arabia-provided-intelligence-on-iran-attack/
[9] https://www.pwc.com/m1/en/services/tax/me-tax-legal-news/2023/uae-israel-cepa.html
[10] https://arabcenterdc.org/resource/saudi-israeli-normalization-and-the-hamas-attack/
[11] https://oec.world/en/profile/bilateral-country/sau/partner/isr
[12] https://carnegieendowment.org/2020/10/15/what-would-happen-if-israel-and-saudi-arabia-established-official-relations-pub-82964
[13] https://apnews.com/article/iran-israel-attacks-

Saudi Arabia and Israel

f27cda966ac274982d968cbcc033eff0

[14] https://www.nbcnews.com/news/mideast/open-secret-saudi-arabia-israel-get-cozy-n821136

[15] https://www.ibanet.org/article/D2659617-4CAB-4FE9-8B60-A971485EC3D6

[16] https://www.reuters.com/world/middle-east/saudis-could-recognise-israel-if-palestinian-issue-resolved-foreign-minister-2024-01-16/

[17] https://cis.mit.edu/publications/analysis-opinion/2023/saudi-israeli-normalization-worth-it

[18] https://www.stateoftelaviv.com/p/reimagining-mid-east-regional-security

[19] https://www.wsj.com/world/middle-east/white-house-makes-fresh-push-for-historic-deal-to-forge-saudi-israel-ties-68ed3a8c

V

Secret Contacts and Covert Cooperation

Covert cooperation and secret contacts have long been essential aspects of the intricate relationship between Saudi Arabia and Israel. While public interactions and diplomatic developments often take center stage, behind-the-scenes collaborations have significantly shaped the engagement between these two nations.

Espionage and Security Cooperation

The realm of espionage and security cooperation serves as a clandestine cornerstone of the Saudi-Israeli relationship. Both countries recognize the value of intelligence sharing in addressing common threats and challenges in the region. Their intelligence agencies, operating discreetly, exchange vital information on issues such as terrorism, regional instability, and the activities of mutual adversaries.

Saudi Arabia and Israel

Saudi Arabia's General Intelligence Presidency (GIP) and Israel's Mossad have developed a covert partnership that transcends ideological barriers, focusing on the security and stability of the region. Through clandestine meetings and secret channels, they share vital intelligence on potential terrorist threats, arms smuggling, and the activities of extremist organizations like Hezbollah and ISIS. This exchange of information allows both countries to take proactive measures to counter these threats more effectively and protect their national security interests.

In addition to information sharing, the intelligence agencies of Saudi Arabia and Israel engage in joint operations targeting shared adversaries. These covert initiatives range from cyber warfare and disruption of enemy communication networks to covert support for opposition groups challenging hostile regimes. By pooling their resources, expertise, and technology, they enhance their capabilities to counter regional threats effectively.

Recognizing the importance of operational coherence and coordination, the intelligence agencies of Saudi Arabia and Israel also invest in joint training programs and simulation exercises. These exercises focus on enhancing communication, interoperability, and crisis response capabilities. Such covert cooperation contributes to a more integrated approach to addressing security challenges, creating a unified front against common enemies.

Shared Interests in Regional Stability

Beneath ideological and cultural differences, Saudi Arabia and Israel share a strong interest in maintaining stability in the Middle East. Their mutual concerns, particularly regarding Iran, have united them in an alignment that transcends public posturing. Covert cooperation between the two nations has become a key component of their relationship to preserve their respective interests and security.

Saudi Arabia and Israel both perceive Iran as a significant threat due to its nuclear aspirations, support for extremist groups, and its regional ambitions. Covert coordination between their intelligence agencies allows for a comprehensive assessment of Iran's activities and intentions. By sharing information on Iran's covert operations, missile development programs, and influence in neighboring countries, they can develop effective strategies to counter Iran's destabilizing actions.

Furthermore, this covert cooperation extends to joint efforts to counteract Iran's support for proxy groups. The intelligence agencies collaborate to monitor financial transactions, arms transfers, and recruitment activities aimed at bolstering Iran's proxy networks. Through covert means, they work to disrupt these channels and neutralize the impact of Iran's proxy warfare across the region.

Additionally, both Saudi Arabia and Israel maintain a keen interest in the peace process between Israel and Palestine. While their public positions may differ, covert cooperation allows them to explore potential avenues for advancing the negotiations behind closed doors. Their shared concerns about extremism and regional stability provide common ground for discreet discussions, promoting confidential dialogue as a means to influence the peace process positively.

Implications for Broader Middle Eastern Dynamics

The covert cooperation between Saudi Arabia and Israel reverberates throughout the entire Middle East region, challenging conventional geopolitical alliances and shifting power dynamics. Their unlikely partnership, rooted in shared interests and mutual threats, has reshaped regional dynamics, influencing conflicts, and presenting potential opportunities for further realignments.

This discreet engagement between Saudi Arabia and Israel has contributed to a broader reassessment of alliances and relationships in the Middle East. Other countries in the region, confronted by similar challenges, are increasingly willing to engage with both Saudi Arabia and Israel covertly, seeking their expertise and intelligence-sharing capabilities. This emerging network of covert cooperation reconfigures the regional balance of power, creating new alignments that cut across traditional fault lines.

However, this evolving covert partnership also carries inherent risks and challenges. The delicate balance of secrecy and disclosure requires careful navigation to avoid unintended consequences. Exposure to their collaboration could lead to backlash and potential destabilization among other regional players. Saudi Arabia and Israel must handle their covert cooperation with caution, preserving the delicate equilibrium they have established.

Understanding the impact of covert cooperation on the wider Middle Eastern landscape is crucial. The in-depth analysis of the evolving Saudi-Israeli relationship, grounded in secret contacts and covert cooperation, sheds light on the complex dynamics at play. It allows for a comprehensive understanding of the true depth and implications of Saudi-Israeli relations for the Middle East and the broader international community.

In the following chapters, further exploration will delve into the interplay between their covert cooperation and ongoing regional conflicts, the potential for open diplomatic relations, and the societal and ethical dimensions of their relationship. This comprehensive examination will provide an in-depth analysis of the evolving alliance and its implications for the Middle East and beyond.

A. ESPIONAGE AND SECURITY COOPERATION

Espionage and security cooperation between Saudi Arabia and Israel have been closely guarded secrets for many years. While public acknowledgment of such activities is rare, numerous reports suggest a deep level of engagement and collaboration in this realm. This chapter delves into the clandestine partnership between these two nations and explores the implications of their cooperation.

One aspect of this relationship involves intelligence sharing. Both countries face common threats and challenges in the region, including terrorist organizations, Iran's influence, and instability in neighboring countries. Saudi Arabia and Israel have established robust channels for sharing information and intelligence, allowing them to pool their resources and knowledge. Such cooperation enables a more comprehensive understanding of regional dynamics and enhances their ability to respond to shared security concerns effectively. By sharing intelligence on potential threats, patterns of extremist activities, and emerging risks, Saudi Arabia and Israel can coordinate their efforts and implement strategies to neutralize threats proactively.

The intelligence sharing between Saudi Arabia and Israel extends beyond conventional methods. Both nations have invested heavily in developing sophisticated cyber capabilities and have established specialized intelligence units dedicated to cyber operations. These units focus on gathering information, disrupting hostile networks, and protecting critical infrastructure. This level of cooperation in cyberspace highlights the growing importance of cyber intelligence in national security strategies. Saudi Arabia and Israel can enhance their cybersecurity and prevent potential cyber-attacks by exchanging information about emerging cyber threats, vulnerabilities, and attack techniques.

Another area of collaboration is in the field of defense. Israel is renowned for its advanced military capabilities, including cutting-edge technology and intelligence systems. Reports suggest that Saudi Arabia has sought to leverage Israel's military expertise to bolster its own defense capabilities. Through covert channels, Saudi Arabia has acquired advanced military equipment and technologies from Israel, including missile defense systems, aerial surveillance systems, and precision-guided munitions. This assistance not only strengthens Saudi Arabia's conventional military capabilities but also contributes to its ability to counter unconventional threats such as ballistic missiles and drones.

Furthermore, Saudi Arabia has benefitted from Israel's vast experience in counterterrorism operations. Israel has a long history of combatting terrorism, dealing with suicide bombings, and foiling terrorist plots. The exchange of knowledge and expertise in this realm is invaluable to Saudi Arabia, which has also faced its fair share of terrorist incidents. By learning from Israel's strategies and tactics, Saudi Arabia can enhance its own counterterrorism capabilities and protect its citizens from extremist threats.

Their cooperation in covert operations extends beyond intelligence sharing and defense procurement. Reports suggest that both countries have engaged in joint operations to counter common threats, including covert airstrikes against Iranian-aligned targets. These strategic covert operations allow Saudi Arabia and Israel to leverage each other's expertise to achieve their security objectives. Additionally, there have been allegations that Israel has provided training and logistical support to Saudi Arabia in its military operations in Yemen, although such claims remain unconfirmed.

The implications of this espionage and security cooperation are significant. It demonstrates a willingness on the part of Saudi Arabia and Israel to prioritize their shared security interests over historical tensions and ideological differences. By pooling their resources and working towards common goals, they have managed to navigate the complex geopolitical landscape of the Middle East and protect their respective national interests.

However, this cooperation also invites criticism and raises ethical questions. Saudi Arabia has been accused of human rights violations and the suppression of dissent, while Israel's actions in the Palestinian territories have drawn international condemnation. The extent to which these issues are considered during their covert collaborations remains uncertain. Balancing strategic interests with humanitarian principles poses a delicate dilemma that both countries must grapple with.

In conclusion, the espionage and security cooperation between Saudi Arabia and Israel is a crucial but clandestine aspect of their relationship. Through intelligence sharing, defense cooperation, and joint operations, they have managed to confront common threats and safeguard their national interests. The developments in cyberspace highlight the importance of cyber intelligence in modern warfare, while the exchange of military capabilities enhances their conventional and unconventional defense capacities. However, ethical concerns and allegations of human rights violations cast shadows over this cooperation, underscoring the complex trade-off between strategic imperatives and international norms. The full extent and implications of their cooperation in this realm will likely remain shrouded in secrecy.

B. SHARED INTERESTS IN REGIONAL STABILITY

Saudi Arabia and Israel

Saudi Arabia and Israel have long been concerned about the stability of the Middle East. Despite their historical differences, both countries share a common interest in promoting regional stability. This chapter will delve into the various ways in which Saudi Arabia and Israel have come together to address this shared concern.

One key area of collaboration between Saudi Arabia and Israel is in countering the influence of Iran. Both countries view Iran as a destabilizing force in the region due to its support for militant groups and its pursuit of nuclear weapons. Saudi Arabia and Israel have engaged in behind-the-scenes cooperation and intelligence sharing to monitor and counter Iran's activities, as well as to develop strategies for containing its influence. They have shared information related to Iran's ballistic missile program, nuclear ambitions, and support for proxy groups such as Hezbollah. This collaborative effort has allowed both countries to have a more comprehensive understanding of Iran's capabilities and intentions, and has served as a deterrent against potential aggressive actions.

Furthermore, Saudi Arabia and Israel have sought to build stronger ties with other countries in the region that share concerns about Iran. The United Arab Emirates, Bahrain, and Sudan have recently normalized relations with Israel, establishing diplomatic ties and opening economic and technological collaborations. This geopolitical shift has created opportunities for greater coordination between Saudi Arabia and Israel, as they work together with these countries to enhance regional security and stability. It also reflects a growing consensus regarding Iran's destabilizing activities and the need for a unified approach to address them.

Terrorism is another significant threat that Saudi Arabia and Israel face, and they have joined forces in combatting this menace. The intelligence agencies of both countries closely cooperate by sharing valuable information on extremist networks, tracking the movements of suspected militants, and coordinating efforts to disrupt terrorist financing. Joint counterterrorism exercises and training programs have been conducted to enhance the capabilities of their security forces. These collaborations have proven to be instrumental in preventing major attacks and dismantling terrorist cells.

In addition to bilateral cooperation, Saudi Arabia and Israel have engaged in multilateral efforts to combat terrorism. They have participated in regional forums, such as the United Nations Counter-Terrorism Center and the Global Coalition to Defeat ISIS, to coordinate efforts with other countries in the fight against terrorism. This multilateral approach allows for a broader scope of intelligence sharing, coordination of military operations, and the pooling of resources to effectively combat the global terrorist threat.

The ongoing conflict in Yemen has also brought Saudi Arabia and Israel closer together. Both countries recognize the potential threats posed by the Houthi rebels, who are backed by Iran and have launched cross-border attacks targeting Saudi Arabia. Israel, too, has concerns about the Houthi's ties to militant groups in the region. Saudi Arabia and Israel have supported the internationally recognized Yemeni government, which is fighting against the Houthis, and have coordinated efforts to stabilize the situation. They have worked together to provide humanitarian aid to the Yemeni people and to encourage a peaceful resolution to the conflict.

Their collaboration in Yemen extends beyond military concerns to include various avenues for humanitarian assistance. Saudi Arabia and Israel have contributed generously to international organizations involved in providing aid to Yemen, such as the United Nations, to alleviate the suffering of the Yemeni people. Their joint efforts include distributing food and medical supplies and supporting the rebuilding of critical infrastructure, contributing to the stability and well-being of Yemen.

Additionally, Saudi Arabia and Israel are mutually interested in maintaining stability in the wider Middle East. They recognize that regional stability is essential for economic growth, international trade, and the well-being of their own populations. Through diplomatic channels, they have collaborated on initiatives to resolve conflicts, promote dialogue, and foster peaceful coexistence. This has included participating in multilateral forums such as the Arab Peace Initiative and engaging with other regional actors to find common ground and build inclusive partnerships.

To further bolster regional stability, Saudi Arabia and Israel have recognized the importance of economic cooperation. Both countries are investing heavily in technology and innovation sectors, aiming to diversify their economies and reduce dependency on oil. This mutual interest in technological advancements has opened doors for collaboration in areas such as cybersecurity, water management, renewable energy, and agri-tech. Joint research and development projects, as well as knowledge sharing, have led to advancements in these fields, benefitting both countries and contributing to the economic stability of the region as a whole.

However, it is important to note that the shared interests of Saudi Arabia and Israel in regional stability have not been without challenges. Historical animosities, competing regional interests, and divergent perspectives on key issues have hindered their cooperation. For Saudi Arabia, public opinion towards Israel remains largely unfavorable due to the ongoing Israeli-Palestinian conflict. Additionally, Saudi Arabia's commitment to pan-Arab causes and its leadership role in the Islamic world makes it cautious about publicly aligning with Israel. Despite these challenges, both countries recognize the importance of working together to address common threats and pursue shared objectives.

Nevertheless, their recognition of the importance of working together, combined with the changing dynamics of the Middle East, has led to increased engagement and a growing recognition of the potential benefits of a closer relationship. As the political landscape of the region shifts, with the United Arab Emirates, Bahrain, and Sudan recently normalizing relations with Israel, the prospects for further cooperation between Saudi Arabia and Israel may improve. This evolving dynamic holds the potential for even deeper collaboration on issues such as technology sharing, energy cooperation, and regional security architecture.

In conclusion, the shared interests of Saudi Arabia and Israel in regional stability have served as a catalyst for their growing collaboration. Countering the influence of Iran, fighting terrorism, addressing the Yemeni crisis, and promoting wider regional stability have brought these countries together, despite their historical differences. Through joint efforts and cooperation, Saudi Arabia and Israel have taken steps towards building trust and finding common ground, with the understanding that stability in the region is vital for their own security and prosperity. Their evolving relationship can shape the Middle East's future dynamics and contribute to a more stable and prosperous region.

C. IMPLICATIONS FOR BROADER MIDDLE EASTERN DYNAMICS

The Saudi-Israeli relationship has far-reaching implications for the broader Middle Eastern region. While historically characterized by tensions and conflicts, recent covert cooperation and shared concerns have paved the way for a potential shift in regional dynamics.

At the heart of these implications lies the Arab-Israeli conflict, an issue that has plagued the region for decades. The conflict has not only caused immense suffering for Palestinians and Israelis but has also contributed to geopolitical instability and hindered regional cooperation. The involvement of Saudi Arabia, a prominent regional power with deep Islamic roots, in pursuing a closer relationship with Israel could potentially reshape the dynamics of this conflict.

Saudi Arabia's historical support for the Palestinians, both politically and financially, has been a defining feature of the Arab-Israeli conflict. However, recent years have witnessed a subtle but significant shift in Saudi Arabia's stance towards Israel. Recognizing the changing dynamics of the region and the need for strategic alliances, Saudi Arabia, under the leadership of Crown Prince Mohammed bin Salman, has sought to build covert ties with Israel.

Several factors have driven this gradual rapprochement. First and foremost, Saudi Arabia recognizes the shared threat posed by Iran. Both Saudi Arabia and Israel view Iran as a regional rival with aggressive foreign policy ambitions, support for proxies, and a pursuit of nuclear weapons. This shared perception of Iran's threat has propelled Saudi Arabia and Israel into deeper cooperation, as they see a united front as essential for countering Iranian influence in the Middle East.

Furthermore, Saudi Arabia's rising concerns over the expansion of radical Islamist movements, particularly those aligned with the Muslim Brotherhood and Shia militias, have also contributed to its recalibration of regional alliances. The kingdom sees Israel as a key partner in combating the influence of these groups, which challenge both Israeli and Saudi interests in the region.

Moreover, Saudi Arabia's recent diplomatic efforts to enhance its global standing have played a role in its approach to Israel. The kingdom seeks to present itself as a progressive and forward-looking nation, and cultivating ties with Israel could reinforce this image. By engaging with Israel, Saudi Arabia aims to break with the traditional Arab narrative of anti-normalization and potentially position itself as a key mediator between Israelis and Palestinians.

The implications of a closer Saudi-Israeli partnership extend beyond the Arab-Israeli conflict. They could significantly impact the broader Middle Eastern geopolitical landscape. In recent years, the Middle East has been marked by a complex web of conflicts and influences, including the Syrian civil war, the Yemen crisis, and the fight against terrorism. Both Saudi Arabia and Israel have been directly or indirectly involved in these conflicts, each pursuing its own regional and security interests.

In Syria, for instance, Saudi Arabia and Israel have had divergent positions regarding the post-war outcome. While Saudi Arabia has supported various armed factions opposing the Assad regime, Israel has primarily focused on preventing the expansion of Iranian-backed militias near its borders. Closer cooperation between Saudi Arabia and Israel could lead to greater coordination in dealing with the Syrian crisis, potentially influencing the geopolitical balance in the region and shaping the outcome of the conflict.

Similarly, in Yemen, Saudi Arabia has been leading a coalition against the Houthi rebels, who are believed to be backed by Iran. Israel has expressed concerns over Iran's influence in Yemen due to its potential to threaten maritime security in the Red Sea, a vital global trade route. The alignment of Saudi Arabia and Israel on the Yemen crisis could result in intensified efforts to counter Iranian activity and support a more unified approach to resolving the conflict.

It is also important to note that Saudi Arabia's potential alignment with Israel could influence other regional players and global powers. Arab states that have historically opposed Israel may feel compelled to reassess their relationships and pursue more pragmatic alliances. This shifting tide could lead to unprecedented opportunities for cooperation, trade, and diplomacy in the region.

The Saudi-Israeli relationship could redefine alliances and geopolitical alignments on the global stage. As Saudi Arabia and Israel forge closer ties, other countries, particularly those that share concerns about Iran or terrorism, may contemplate developing stronger relationships with both nations. This realignment of global powers could have significant consequences for the balance of power in the international arena.

However, the implications of a closer Saudi-Israeli relationship are not without challenges and potential obstacles. Deep-rooted historical and religious animosities, both within domestic populations and the wider Muslim world, pose a significant hurdle. The Palestinian issue, which remains at the heart of the Arab-Israeli conflict, continues to evoke strong emotions and trigger vehement reactions. Overt normalization of relations between Saudi Arabia and Israel could be met with resistance and backlash from segments of society that view Israel as an occupying force and an oppressor of Palestinians.

Striking a balance between pursuing strategic partnerships and upholding fundamental humanitarian principles is an ethical dilemma that cannot be ignored. Both Saudi Arabia and Israel have faced criticism for their human rights records and their treatment of minority populations. The international community must carefully navigate these complexities, encouraging progress on human rights while recognizing the potential benefits of closer Saudi-Israeli ties in addressing regional challenges.

In conclusion, the implications of the Saudi-Israeli relationship for broader Middle Eastern dynamics are significant and multifaceted. A closer alignment between these two regional powers has the potential to reshape the Arab-Israeli conflict, challenge Iran's influence, impact ongoing regional conflicts, and redefine regional and global alliances. However, these implications must be considered in light of the challenges posed by historical tensions, societal backlash, and ethical dilemmas. Navigating these complexities will be crucial in harnessing the potential benefits of closer Saudi-Israeli ties while ensuring regional stability, human rights respect, and a more peaceful and prosperous Middle East.

In a Nutshell

A. Espionage and Security Cooperation

Espionage and security cooperation between Saudi Arabia and Israel have been pivotal, albeit covert, elements of their relationship. This cooperation has often involved the exchange of sophisticated spy systems and intelligence sharing. For instance, Israel sold approximately $250 million worth of sophisticated spy systems to Saudi Arabia, which included the transfer of Israeli espionage equipment. This indicates a deep level of trust and cooperation in security matters, which is not publicly acknowledged due to the sensitive nature of their diplomatic standings.

Moreover, the NSO Group, an Israeli firm, has been involved in selling Pegasus spyware to Saudi Arabia. This tool has been used for various intelligence purposes, demonstrating an ongoing partnership in cybersecurity and surveillance. These interactions underscore a significant aspect of the covert relationship, focusing on enhancing each country's security capabilities against common threats.

B. Shared Interests in Regional Stability

Saudi Arabia and Israel share a fundamental interest in maintaining regional stability, primarily due to the mutual threat they perceive from Iran. This shared concern has fostered a strategic albeit unofficial alliance. Both nations have engaged in intelligence sharing about Iran's activities, which has been crucial for Israel's security operations and Saudi Arabia's strategic positioning in the region.

The stability of the Middle East is also a significant concern for both countries as it directly impacts their national security and economic interests. For instance, both nations have been involved in discussions and possibly cooperation on various regional security matters, including the threats posed by non-state actors like Hezbollah and the Houthi rebels, which are seen as proxies of Iran. This cooperation not only helps in countering immediate threats but also in strategizing for long-term regional stability.

C. Implications for Broader Middle Eastern Dynamics

The covert cooperation between Saudi Arabia and Israel has broader implications for Middle Eastern dynamics. It challenges the traditional political alignments in the region and could potentially reshape the geopolitical landscape. For example, the potential normalization of relations between Saudi Arabia and Israel, as seen through various secret negotiations and security collaborations, could lead to a new strategic realignment in the Middle East.

This evolving relationship might also influence other Arab countries' stances towards Israel, as seen with the Abraham Accords, where UAE and Bahrain normalized relations with Israel. Saudi Arabia's potential move towards formalizing relations with Israel could encourage other nations to reconsider their positions, thereby altering the traditional Arab-Israeli dynamics.

Furthermore, the cooperation between these two countries could set a precedent for how Middle Eastern nations address shared threats and cooperate on security issues, potentially leading to a more integrated approach to regional security and stability. This could also impact the Palestinian issue, as Saudi Arabia has historically advocated for a Palestinian state, and its closer ties with Israel might influence future negotiations and peace processes.

In conclusion, the covert interactions between Saudi Arabia and Israel, particularly in espionage and security cooperation, not only highlight their shared interests in regional stability but also have significant implications for the broader Middle Eastern dynamics. These developments could potentially lead to a new era of Middle Eastern geopolitics, where old rivalries are reassessed in light of emerging regional and global challenges.

Sources and References

[1] https://www.orsam.org.tr/en/from-regional-isolation-to-engagement-exploring-the-prospects-of-saudi-israel-normalization/

[2] https://www.trtworld.com/middle-east/the-eight-arab-states-that-openly-and-unabashedly-deal-with-israel-33551

[3] https://www.brookings.edu/articles/the-emergence-of-gcc-israel-relations-in-a-changing-middle-east/

[4] https://apps.dtic.mil/sti/trecms/pdf/AD1165033.pdf

[5] https://scholarworks.wmich.edu/cgi/viewcontent.cgi?article=4021&context=honors_theses

[6] https://www.unav.edu/en/web/global-affairs/secret-diplomacy-in-the-middle-east-negotiations-for-saudi-arabia-normalization-of-relations-with-israel

[7] https://themedialine.org/top-stories/normalization-puzzle-the-complex-path-toward-israel-saudi-arabia-rapprochement/

[8] https://www.atlanticcouncil.org/blogs/iransource/regional-stability-is-in-the-interest-of-both-saudi-arabia-and-iran/

[9] https://carnegieendowment.org/2020/10/15/what-would-happen-if-israel-and-saudi-arabia-established-official-relations-pub-82964

[10] https://www.theguardian.com/world/2021/jul/20/pegasus-project-turns-spotlight-on-spyware-firm-nso-ties-to-israeli-state

[11] https://www.atlanticcouncil.org/blogs/menasource/saudi-arabia-israel-two-state-gaza-normalization/

[12] https://www.chathamhouse.org/2023/03/abraham-accords-and-israel-uae-normalization/03-security-landscape

[13] https://en.wikipedia.org/wiki/Mossad

[14] https://www.fpri.org/article/2024/03/the-realignment-of-the-middle-east/
[15] https://carnegieendowment.org/sada/91187
[16] https://www.defensenews.com/opinion/2024/04/18/us-israeli-arab-coordination-in-mideast-against-iran-comes-to-fruition/
[17] https://carnegieendowment.org/2023/10/13/arab-perspectives-on-middle-east-crisis-pub-90774
[18] https://www.timesofisrael.com/giving-unheard-of-assent-to-saudi-nuclearization-israel-girds-for-cold-war-with-iran/
[19] https://jpost.com/middle-east/report-israel-sold-250m-of-sophisticated-spy-systems-to-saudi-arabia-570539
[20] https://onlinelibrary.wiley.com/doi/10.1111/mepo.12731?af=R

VI

Regional Conflicts and Struggles

Impact of the Arab-Israeli Conflict

The Arab-Israeli conflict, a protracted dispute rooted in competing national aspirations and territorial claims, has had a far-reaching impact on the dynamics of the Middle East and Saudi-Israeli relations. Historically, Saudi Arabia has been a steadfast supporter of the Palestinian cause, empathizing with their plight and advocating for their rights in the occupied territories. This perspective has often shaped the Kingdom's approach towards Israel, perceiving it as an oppressor of the Palestinians.

The Arab-Israeli conflict has further strained Saudi-Israeli relations due to their differing stances on key issues, such as the status of Jerusalem, the right of return for Palestinian refugees, and the establishment of an independent Palestinian state. Saudi Arabia has consistently condemned Israeli actions in the occupied territories and supported various peace initiatives aimed at resolving the conflict through negotiation and a two-state solution.

However, there have been some noteworthy changes in Saudi Arabia's approach to the conflict in recent years. Under the leadership of Crown Prince Mohammed bin Salman, the Kingdom has shown signs of a more pragmatic stance. Recognizing the shifting dynamics in the region and the continued deadlock in Palestinian-Israeli negotiations, Saudi Arabia has sought to explore avenues for closer ties with Israel based on shared strategic interests.

Saudi-Iran Rivalry and Israel's Strategic Position

The longstanding rivalry between Saudi Arabia and Iran, fueled by sectarian and geopolitical differences, adds complexity to Saudi-Israeli relations. Both Saudi Arabia and Israel view Iran as a major regional threat due to its pursuit of nuclear weapons, its support for militant groups, and its ambition to expand its influence throughout the Middle East. This common concern has fostered a certain degree of alignment between Saudi Arabia and Israel, as they perceive Iran's activities as destabilizing and seek to counter its influence.

While there is no formal diplomatic relationship between Saudi Arabia and Israel, there have been reports of discreet cooperation and intelligence sharing to address shared challenges posed by Iran and its proxies. The strategic position of Israel in the region, as a technologically advanced military power and a key ally of the United States, further influences Saudi Arabia's calculus in dealing with the complex Saudi-Iran rivalry. Despite their differences, both countries recognize the importance of regional stability and containment of Iranian influence.

Role in Current Geopolitical Upheavals

The Middle East has witnessed significant geopolitical upheavals in recent years, with conflicts in Syria, Yemen, and Iraq exacerbating regional tensions and threatening stability on multiple fronts. These conflicts have shaped the evolving landscape of Saudi-Israeli relations in various ways.

In Yemen, where a Saudi-led coalition is fighting against Houthi rebels supported by Iran, Saudi Arabia finds itself on the opposite side of the conflict from Israel. This divergence in interests is driven by regional power dynamics and the pursuit of strategic objectives. However, both Saudi Arabia and Israel are united by their concerns about extremist groups and the potential for chaos and instability to spill over into neighboring countries.

The Syrian conflict has also influenced Saudi-Israeli relations, indirectly creating opportunities for discreet cooperation given their shared interest in countering Iran's growing presence in the region. While Saudi Arabia has supported various rebel factions seeking regime change in Syria, Israel has focused primarily on preventing the transfer of advanced weapons to Hezbollah, an Iranian-backed Lebanese militant group. This intersecting interest has occasionally resulted in unacknowledged coordination between the two countries.

Moreover, Israel's strategic position has been a factor of consideration for Saudi Arabia and other regional actors. Countries such as the United Arab Emirates and Bahrain have recently established diplomatic ties and normalized relations with Israel, a development that has reshaped the dynamics of the Arab-Israeli conflict and set the stage for potential shifts in regional alliances.

The COVID-19 pandemic has also had implications for Saudi-Israeli relations, as the virus and its economic fallout have created new challenges in the region. While the pandemic has strained global economies and diverted attention away from geopolitical conflicts, it has also presented opportunities for increased cooperation. The need for medical supplies, expertise, and economic recovery has prompted some informal channels of communication and cooperation between Saudi Arabia and Israel.

In conclusion, a deeper analysis of regional conflicts and struggles highlights the intricate web of factors influencing Saudi-Israeli relations. The Arab-Israeli conflict, the Saudi-Iran rivalry, evolving regional power dynamics, and recent geopolitical upheavals all contribute to the delicate balance between cooperation and tension between the two countries. Understanding these complexities is essential to comprehending the broader implications for regional stability, global diplomacy, and the pursuit of lasting peace in the Middle East.

A. IMPACT OF THE ARAB-ISRAELI CONFLICT

The Arab-Israeli conflict has had a profound and multifaceted impact on Saudi-Israeli relations throughout history. This chapter delves into the complexities, consequences, and dynamics of this long-standing conflict and its implications for the relationship between Saudi Arabia and Israel.

The roots of the Arab-Israeli conflict can be traced back to the early 20th century when the Zionist movement emerged with the aim of establishing a Jewish homeland in Palestine. This vision clashed with the aspirations of the Arab population living in Palestine, leading to escalating tensions between the two communities. In 1947, the United Nations proposed a partition plan to divide Palestine into separate Jewish and Arab states. While the Jewish community accepted the plan, the Arab nations, including Saudi Arabia, rejected it, viewing it as an infringement on the rights of

Saudi Arabia and Israel

the Palestinian people. This rejection marked the beginning of a series of conflicts and deepened the animosity between the Arab states and Israel.

The establishment of the State of Israel in 1948 further intensified the Arab-Israeli conflict and led to the displacement of hundreds of thousands of Palestinians. Arab nations, including Saudi Arabia, rallied to support their Palestinian brethren, viewing the creation of Israel as an injustice and a violation of international agreements. Saudi Arabia, along with other Arab states, declared war on Israel, setting off the first Arab-Israeli war.

Over the years, the conflict has evolved and witnessed several major wars and numerous smaller-scale conflicts. The Six-Day War in 1967 and the Yom Kippur War in 1973 significantly impacted the Arab-Israeli conflict and deepened the divide between the parties involved. For Saudi Arabia, supporting the Palestinian cause became a central component of its regional policy, advocating for the right to self-determination and sovereignty for the Palestinian people.

The impact of the Arab-Israeli conflict on Saudi-Israeli relations has been substantial. The Israeli occupation of Palestinian territories, particularly the West Bank and Gaza Strip, has been a constant source of tension, with Saudi Arabia vehemently condemning Israeli policies and actions in these areas. As a result, official diplomatic relations between Saudi Arabia and Israel have remained non-existent despite reports of behind-the-scenes cooperation between the two countries on certain security and intelligence matters.

However, recent years have witnessed a shift in attitudes among some Arab nations, including Saudi Arabia, regarding Israel and the Arab-Israeli conflict. Growing concerns over Iran's regional ambitions and the shared fight against terrorism have prompted some Arab states to explore the possibility of normalization with Israel. This new discourse has been fueled by strategic considerations, with countries like Saudi Arabia recognizing that a closer relationship with Israel could serve as a counterbalance to Iranian influence in the region.

Moreover, the Arab League, established in 1945 to coordinate Arab states' efforts against Israel, has shown signs of fragmentation regarding the Arab-Israeli conflict. While the league has maintained the official position of supporting Palestinian rights and opposing Israeli occupation, there have been instances where individual member states have pursued more pragmatic approaches to engage with Israel at various levels. This divergence within the Arab League has further complicated the relationship between Saudi Arabia and Israel, as each country navigates its own path within the broader regional dynamics.

The economic consequences of the Arab-Israeli conflict have also been significant. Arab nations implemented boycotts and economic sanctions against Israel early on, severely limiting trade and economic interactions. These measures hindered potential economic cooperation between Saudi Arabia, Israel, and other Arab states, affecting regional trade and development. However, in recent years, some countries, including the United Arab Emirates and Bahrain, have signed normalization agreements with Israel, opening up possibilities for increased economic ties and collaborations.

Saudi Arabia has also played a role in broader regional dynamics concerning the Arab-Israeli conflict. The kingdom has participated in various Israeli-Palestinian peace negotiations, attempting to mediate and facilitate dialogue between the two parties. Saudi Arabia's involvement reflects its desire for a peaceful resolution and stability in the region, as well as its recognition of the need for a comprehensive settlement that addresses the legitimate aspirations of both Israelis and Palestinians.

In conclusion, the Arab-Israeli conflict has left a lasting impact on Saudi-Israeli relations, shaping the regional policies, alliances, and foreign policy decision-making of both countries. While traditional obstacles to official diplomatic ties remain, the changing dynamics of the conflict and shared strategic interests have provided opportunities for potential shifts in attitudes and approaches. Understanding the complexities, consequences, and evolving dynamics of the Arab-Israeli conflict is critical to comprehending the dynamics of Saudi-Israeli relations and the potential for future developments.

B. SAUDI-IRAN RIVALRY AND ISRAEL'S STRATEGIC POSITION

- **Historical Roots of the Saudi-Iran Rivalry**
    - The rivalry between Saudi Arabia and Iran has deep historical roots dating back centuries. Understanding the historical context is essential to fully grasp the complex dynamics between these regional powers and Israel's strategic positioning.
    - Sectarian Divisions: Sunni-Shia Divide The division between Sunni and Shia Islam plays a significant role in the Saudi-Iran rivalry. Saudi Arabia, the birthplace of Islam, is predominantly Sunni, while Iran is the largest Shia-majority country. The sectarian divide has historically fuelled tensions and power struggles between these two Muslim sects.
    - Competing Visions of Regional Leadership Saudi Arabia and Iran have competing visions of regional leadership. Saudi Arabia, as the custodian of the Two Holy Mosques in Mecca and Medina, sees itself as the

rightful leader of the Muslim world. At the same time, Iran seeks to establish itself as the champion of Shia Muslims globally. These competing aspirations have created a constant power struggle between the two countries.

- ○ Historical Conflicts and Tensions Throughout history, Saudi Arabia and Iran have experienced various conflicts and tensions. Historical events have shaped the Saudi-Iran rivalry from the Iranian Revolution in 1979, which established the Islamic Republic and challenged Saudi Arabia's conservative monarchy, to disputes over regional influence in Lebanon, Iraq, and Bahrain.

- **Impact of the Arab-Israeli Conflict**
  - ○ The Arab-Israeli conflict significantly impacts the Saudi-Iran rivalry and Israel's strategic position in the Middle East. Understanding this influence is crucial for analyzing the complex dynamics between these regional powers.
  - ○ Saudi Arabia's Support for the Palestinian Cause Saudi Arabia, along with other Arab states, has historically championed the Palestinian cause, supporting their quest for an independent state. This support stems from religious, moral, and political reasons, as the Palestinian issue holds immense significance for the wider Arab and Muslim world. The Kingdom has provided financial aid to the Palestinian Authority and reiterated its commitment to the Arab Peace Initiative, which calls for a two-state solution.
  - ○ Iranian Backing of Palestinian Armed Groups Iran has provided financial, military, and ideological support to various Palestinian armed groups, notably Hamas and Islamic Jihad. This backing serves Iran's interests in

undermining Israel and bolstering its influence in the region. It exacerbates tensions between Saudi Arabia and Iran, as they find themselves on opposing sides of the Arab-Israeli conflict. Iran's support for these groups also poses a challenge to Israel's security and peace efforts.

- Implications for Israel's Security and Regional Dynamics The Arab-Israeli conflict directly impacts Israel's security and regional dynamics. The ongoing tensions and violence create an unpredictable landscape for Israel, requiring constant vigilance and strategic planning. The rivalry between Saudi Arabia and Iran adds layer of complexity to this already volatile situation. Israel must navigate this landscape by considering the potential security threats both sides pose while strategically leveraging any shared interests. Israel also aims to build strategic alliances with countries like Saudi Arabia that share concerns about Iran's regional influence.

- **Proxy Wars and Regional Power Struggles**
  - Proxy wars and regional power struggles between Saudi Arabia and Iran further complicate the strategic landscape for Israel. Analyzing these conflicts sheds light on the intricate dynamics that impact Israel's security and regional positioning.
  - Yemen Conflict: Saudi Arabia vs Iran-backed Houthi Rebels The ongoing conflict in Yemen is a prime example of the proxy war between Saudi Arabia and Iran. Saudi Arabia leads a multinational coalition supporting the internationally recognized Yemeni government, while Iran provides backing to Houthi rebels. This conflict highlights the intensifying regional power rivalry

and potential implications for Israel's security. Israel closely monitors the situation, concerned about Iran's expanding influence in its southern neighbor and the potential threat it poses to its maritime trade routes through the Red Sea and the strategic Bab el-Mandeb Strait.

- Syria Crisis: Rival Support for Different Factions The Syrian civil war has witnessed both Saudi Arabia and Iran backing different factions. Saudi Arabia has supported rebel groups seeking to overthrow the Assad regime, while Iran has provided military and financial aid to Syria's government. These competing interests have made Syria a crucial battleground for regional influence, with Israel closely monitoring the situation. Israel has conducted airstrikes in Syria to prevent the transfer of advanced weapons to Hezbollah and other Iranian-backed forces, aiming to protect its own security interests and prevent the entrenchment of Iranian forces near its borders.
- Lebanon's Hezbollah: Iranian Influence vs Israeli Threat Perception Hezbollah, the Iran-backed Lebanese militant group, poses a significant challenge to Israel's security. While Iran supports Hezbollah's operations against Israel, Saudi Arabia and its allies consider the group a regional threat due to its direct engagement in conflicts across the region. This divergence further illustrates the complexities Israel faces in navigating the Saudi-Iran rivalry. Israel maintains a strong military presence along its northern border with Lebanon, monitoring Hezbollah's activities while also engaging in intelligence and diplomatic efforts to counter Iran's influence.

- Iraq's Struggle for Stability: Saudi Influence vs Iranian Intervention Iraq's political landscape has been heavily influenced by the rivalry between Saudi Arabia and Iran. Following the U.S. invasion in 2003, Iran capitalized on the power vacuum and established significant influence over Iraq's Shia-dominated government. Saudi Arabia, concerned about Iranian encroachment, has sought to counterbalance Iran's influence by supporting Sunni factions and engaging in diplomatic and economic outreach. Israel closely observes these dynamics, acknowledging that a stable and sovereign Iraq is crucial for regional stability and its own security interests.

C. ROLE IN CURRENT GEOPOLITICAL UPHEAVALS

The geopolitical upheavals in the Middle East have posed significant challenges and created opportunities for regional actors to shape the evolving dynamics. Saudi Arabia and Israel, two key players in the region, have found themselves navigating the complexities of this landscape. This extended chapter delves deeper into their respective roles in countering Iran's influence, involvement in the Syrian conflict, managing the Israeli-Palestinian conflict, and cooperation in addressing terrorism and extremism.

Countering Iran's Influence:

Iran's regional ambitions and assertive foreign policy have raised concerns in both Saudi Arabia and Israel. As the dominant Shiite power in the region, Iran has sought to expand its influence by supporting militant groups and engaging in proxy wars, creating tensions with their Sunni-majority neighbors.

Saudi Arabia, as a leading Sunni power, has established itself as a counterweight to Iran's influence in the region. The Kingdom has formed alliances with like-minded countries and non-state actors to counter Iran's proxies. Bahrain, for instance, hosts the U.S. Fifth Fleet and houses a substantial Saudi military presence, allowing both countries to monitor and respond to Iranian activities in the Persian Gulf.

Moreover, Saudi Arabia has been proactive in creating regional alliances to consolidate efforts against Iran. The Islamic Military Counterterrorism Coalition (IMCTC), led by Saudi Arabia, was established in 2015 and brings together 41 Muslim-majority countries to combat terrorism and extremist ideologies, further bolstering Saudi Arabia's position as a regional player in countering Iran's influence.

Saudi Arabia has also been actively supporting Sunni groups in countries where Iran has exerted influence, such as Iraq, Syria, and Lebanon. The Kingdom's financial aid and political support have aimed to bolster Sunni groups and strengthen their position against Iranian-backed Shiite militias. In Iraq, for example, Saudi Arabia has offered assistance to Sunni tribal militias fighting against ISIS and Iranian-backed Shiite militias, aiming to counterbalance Iran's growing influence.

The shared opposition to Iranian-backed Hezbollah in Lebanon has particularly highlighted the convergence of interests between Saudi Arabia and Israel. Both countries perceive Hezbollah's dominance in Lebanon as a threat to regional stability and have sought various means to limit its influence. Indirect cooperation, primarily through back-channel communications, has enabled the two countries to exchange intelligence and coordinate efforts to undermine and mitigate the impact of Hezbollah.

Israel, on the other hand, has viewed Iran as an existential threat due to its rhetoric against the Jewish state and support for Palestinian militant groups. The Israeli government has consistently opposed Iran's nuclear program and has deployed various covert and overt measures to impede its progress. Close cooperation with intelligence agencies from countries such as Saudi Arabia has played a significant role in gathering information regarding Iran's nuclear program and other activities.

Furthermore, Israel has engaged in a covert campaign against Iranian targets in Syria, aiming to disrupt Iran's military buildup and weapons transfers to Hezbollah. This campaign has involved numerous airstrikes, targeting Iranian personnel and infrastructure, often going unclaimed but widely attributed to Israel. The alignment of interests between Saudi Arabia and Israel in countering Iran has provided opportunities for clandestine cooperation.

Involvement in the Syrian Conflict:

The Syrian conflict, which erupted in 2011, has drawn regional and international actors into a complex web of alliances and rivalries. Both Saudi Arabia and Israel have been active participants, albeit with different motivations, in shaping the outcome of the conflict.

Saudi Arabia's involvement in the Syrian conflict revolves around countering Iranian influence and seeking to install a Sunni-dominated government in Syria. The Kingdom has provided significant financial and military support to various opposition groups to overthrow President Bashar al-Assad, whom they regard as a key ally of Iran. Despite setbacks, including the resurgence of government forces and the intervention of Russia, Saudi Arabia remains committed to supporting anti-Assad forces.

Saudi Arabia's support for anti-Assad forces has focused on military and humanitarian aid. The Kingdom has been one of the largest contributors to relief efforts, providing aid to millions of internally displaced Syrians and hosting refugee populations. This approach aims to maintain influence among the opposition and win the hearts and minds of the Syrian people while countering Iran's narrative of supporting the Assad regime.

Israel's concerns in the Syrian conflict transcend its rivalry with Iran. The Israeli government has closely monitored the transfer of advanced weapons from Iran to Hezbollah, mainly via Syrian territory. Israel's airstrikes in Syria have specifically targeted Iranian-backed facilities, arms convoys, and military installations, aiming to disrupt Iranian arms smuggling networks. By doing so, Israel seeks to safeguard its security and prevent the strengthening of its adversaries.

Moreover, Israeli involvement has also been driven by the need to maintain a buffer zone against potential threats from radicalized Islamist groups operating in Syria, such as ISIS and al-Qaeda affiliates. Israel has provided medical aid and humanitarian assistance to Syrians affected by the conflict, seeking to foster a positive image and build alliances with moderate forces that oppose both Assad and extremist groups.

Although their objectives in Syria differ, Saudi Arabia and Israel have shared an interest in countering Iranian influence and preventing the consolidation of pro-Iranian forces. This has created opportunities for tacit coordination and discreet communication between the two countries to avoid direct clashes and ensure their actions do not hinder each other's objectives.

Managing the Israeli-Palestinian Conflict:

The Israeli-Palestinian conflict remains a central issue in regional geopolitics, with profound implications for Saudi Arabia and Israel. While their positions on the conflict differ, both countries have recognized the importance of finding a resolution for regional stability.

Saudi Arabia has been a longstanding supporter of the Palestinian cause, advocating for a Palestinian state based on the pre-1967 borders with East Jerusalem as its capital. The Kingdom has exerted diplomatic pressure on Israel and has attempted to unify Arab states around a peace initiative known as the Arab Peace Initiative, which offers normalized relations with Israel in exchange for a just resolution to the conflict.

In recent years, there have been notable shifts in Saudi Arabia's approach to the Israeli-Palestinian conflict. Crown Prince Mohammed bin Salman's rise to power has brought about a more pragmatic stance, emphasizing the region's need for cooperation and economic development. While not abandoning the Palestinians, Saudi Arabia has acknowledged the importance of engaging with Israel on issues of mutual concern, such as countering Iran and fostering regional stability.

Although overt cooperation between Saudi Arabia and Israel in addressing the Israeli-Palestinian conflict remains politically sensitive and challenging, there have been reports of clandestine engagements between the two countries. These behind-the-scenes communications have explored potential peace and regional stability avenues, recognizing the shared interest in countering common security threats.

Israel, for its part, has taken steps to normalize relations with other Arab countries, including the United Arab Emirates, Bahrain, Sudan, and Morocco. These developments offer a glimmer of hope for potential normalization with Saudi Arabia in the future, leading to a more comprehensive and stable resolution to the Israeli-Palestinian conflict.

Cooperation in Addressing Terrorism and Extremism:

The rise of non-state actors, the collapse of state institutions, and the spread of extremist ideologies have presented shared challenges for Saudi Arabia and Israel. Both countries have recognized the need to cooperate in countering terrorist organizations and addressing the underlying conditions that fuel extremism.

Saudi Arabia has actively participated in regional security coalitions, such as the Global Coalition to Defeat ISIS, and has implemented robust counterterrorism measures at both the domestic and regional levels. The Kingdom has taken a proactive approach to combating extremist ideologies, recognizing the importance of addressing the root causes of radicalization.

In recent years, Saudi Arabia has embarked on a series of domestic reforms aimed at promoting moderation and countering extremist ideologies. These reforms have included measures such as cracking down on financing extremist groups, establishing rehabilitation programs for former extremists, and implementing educational reforms to promote tolerance and moderation.

Saudi Arabia has also been at the forefront of countering online radicalization and propaganda. The Kingdom has established the Saudi National Cybersecurity Authority (NCA) to monitor and combat extremist content online. Additionally, Saudi Arabia has cooperated with international partners, including Israel, in sharing information and intelligence to disrupt terrorist networks and prevent attacks.

Israel, on the other hand, has extensive experience in combating terrorism and has developed sophisticated counterterrorism strategies. The country faces threats from various extremist groups, including Hamas and Hezbollah, as well as from lone-wolf attacks inspired by radical ideologies.

Israel's counterterrorism efforts have focused on intelligence gathering, preemptive strikes against potential threats, and security measures to protect its population. The country has utilized its advanced intelligence capabilities to preempt and disrupt terrorist activities. It often relies on close cooperation with partner countries, including Saudi Arabia, to share intelligence and coordinate efforts.

Furthermore, Israel has developed cutting-edge technology and expertise in cyber defense, which has become increasingly crucial in countering online radicalization and cyber threats. Israel has actively shared its cybersecurity knowledge with partner countries, including Saudi Arabia, to enhance their capabilities in countering the evolving terrorist threat landscape.

The convergence of interests between Saudi Arabia and Israel in countering terrorism and extremism has provided a foundation for cooperation in various domains. While this cooperation may often occur behind closed doors, it demonstrates the recognition of shared challenges and the importance of working together to address them effectively.

Conclusion

Saudi Arabia and Israel have found themselves navigating complex geopolitical landscapes that have been shaped by Iran's regional ambitions, the Syrian conflict, the Israeli-Palestinian conflict, and the rise of terrorism and extremism. While their positions on certain issues may differ, there are areas of convergence that have created opportunities for cooperation and coordination.

Both countries perceive Iran as a common adversary and have actively sought to counter its regional influence. This shared objective has led to discreet cooperation in various domains, including intelligence sharing, countering Hezbollah's influence, and disrupting Iran's military buildup.

In the Syrian conflict, Saudi Arabia and Israel have pursued different objectives, but their actions have been driven by the need to safeguard their security and prevent the consolidation of pro-Iranian forces. This has created opportunities for tacit coordination and discreet communication to ensure their actions align without hindering each other's overall objectives.

The Israeli-Palestinian conflict remains a central issue in the region. While Saudi Arabia and Israel may have differing positions, there have been efforts to explore potential avenues for peace and regional stability. The recent normalization agreements between Israel and other Arab countries offer hope for potential normalization with Saudi Arabia in the future.

Both Saudi Arabia and Israel recognize the importance of cooperation in countering terrorism and extremism. They have pursued robust counterterrorism measures, including intelligence sharing, cybersecurity cooperation, and countering online radicalization. The convergence of interests in this domain has laid the groundwork for cooperation and coordination in addressing shared challenges.

In conclusion, Saudi Arabia's and Israel's roles in the current geopolitical upheavals reflect the complexities and fluidity of the regional landscape. While their interests and approaches may vary, areas of overlap provide opportunities for cooperation and coordination, ultimately contributing to regional stability and security.

In a Nutshell

A. Impact of the Arab-Israeli Conflict

The Arab-Israeli conflict has had a profound impact on the unofficial ties between Saudi Arabia and Israel. Historically, Saudi Arabia has been a staunch supporter of the Palestinian cause, which has been a significant barrier to open diplomatic relations with Israel. The kingdom's public stance has often necessitated a balancing act, supporting Palestinian statehood while also engaging in covert cooperation with Israel against mutual threats.

The recent conflicts, particularly the Gaza war, have put Saudi Arabia in a delicate position. While there is a strategic alignment with Israel, especially against Iran, Saudi Arabia must also consider the sentiments of its population and the broader Arab world, which remains largely sympathetic to the Palestinian cause. This dynamic was evident when Saudi Arabia appointed its first ambassador to the Palestinians, signaling its continued support for their statehood, which remains a precondition for formalizing ties with Israel.

B. Saudi-Iran Rivalry and Israel's Strategic Position

The rivalry between Saudi Arabia and Iran is a central element shaping the covert cooperation with Israel. Both Saudi Arabia and Israel view Iran as a significant threat, particularly regarding Iran's nuclear ambitions and its support for proxy groups in the region such as Hezbollah and the Houthis. This shared threat perception has driven Saudi-Israeli intelligence sharing and strategic cooperation, albeit discreetly.

The recent détente between Saudi Arabia and Iran, brokered by China, introduces new complexities into the Saudi-Israeli relationship. While it might reduce immediate regional tensions, it also causes concern in Israel about the potential for Saudi-Iranian rapprochement to limit Israeli strategic options or lead to a reduction in covert support from Saudi Arabia. This evolving scenario forces Israel to recalibrate its regional strategy, balancing its covert alliances with the changing dynamics of Saudi-Iranian relations.

C. Role in Current Geopolitical Upheavals

Saudi Arabia and Israel play significant roles in the current geopolitical upheavals across the Middle East. The shifting alliances and the normalization of relations between Israel and several Arab states under the Abraham Accords have altered the regional landscape. These accords, which Saudi Arabia has tacitly supported but not joined, signify a potential shift towards a more integrated Middle Eastern bloc that could counterbalance Iranian influence.

Moreover, the involvement of external powers like the United States and China plays a crucial role. The U.S. continues to be a major player in Middle Eastern politics, pushing for further normalization between Israel and Arab states, including Saudi Arabia. At the same time, China's increasing influence, particularly through its economic investments and diplomatic initiatives like the Saudi-Iran rapprochement, introduces a new layer of complexity.

In summary, the unofficial ties between Saudi Arabia and Israel are significantly influenced by the broader Arab-Israeli conflict, the Saudi-Iran rivalry, and the ongoing geopolitical upheavals in the region. These factors collectively shape the strategic calculations of both nations, driving them towards covert cooperation despite the lack of formal diplomatic relations.

Sources and References

[1] https://www.foreignaffairs.com/united-states/case-against-israeli-saudi-deal

[2] https://scholarworks.wmich.edu/cgi/viewcontent.cgi?article=4021&context=honors_theses

[3] https://breakingdefense.com/2023/03/improved-saudi-iran-relationship-has-israel-nervous-about-iran-and-about-china/

[4] https://www.brookings.edu/articles/how-to-understand-israel-and-saudi-arabias-secretive-relationship/

[5] https://www.brookings.edu/articles/the-emergence-of-gcc-israel-relations-in-a-changing-middle-east/

[6] https://www.brookings.edu/articles/the-new-geopolitics-of-the-middle-east-americas-role-in-a-changing-region/

[7] https://www.washingtoninstitute.org/policy-analysis/palestinians-surprisingly-split-saudi-israel-normalization

[8] https://www.foreignaffairs.com/middle-east/what-war-gaza-israel-means-saudi-arabia

[9] https://www.theguardian.com/world/2024/apr/19/gulf-states-response-to-iran-israel-conflict-may-decide-outcome-of-crisis

[10] https://www.newarab.com/analysis/how-saudi-arabia-approaching-israels-war-gaza

[11] https://www.prio.org/publications/13761

[12] https://www.reuters.com/world/middle-east/saudi-arabia-says-there-will-be-no-diplomatic-relations-with-israel-without-an-2024-02-07/

[13] https://carnegieendowment.org/2020/10/15/what-would-happen-if-israel-and-saudi-arabia-established-official-relations-pub-82964

[14] https://www.aljazeera.com/news/2023/9/21/whats-happening-with-normalising-ties-between-saudi-arabia-and-israel

[15] https://www.tandfonline.com/doi/full/10.1080/25765949.2023.2299076

[16] https://world101.cfr.org/rotw/middle-east/geopolitics

[17] https://www.atlanticcouncil.org/blogs/iransource/israel-iran-escalation-syria-zahedi/

[18] https://www.foreignaffairs.com/middle-east/what-saudi-israeli-deal-could-mean-palestinians

[19] https://www.worldpoliticsreview.com/israel-iran-saudi-arabia-battle-for-supremacy-in-the-middle-east/

[20] https://www.lemonde.fr/en/international/article/2024/04/18/the-balancing-act-of-the-gulf-states-in-the-face-off-between-israel-and-iran_6668827_4.html

VII

Prospects

The future prospects for Saudi-Israeli relations are both intriguing and complex. While there have been hints of a potential rapprochement between the two countries, significant challenges and obstacles still remain. This chapter explores the various factors at play and analyzes the potential paths that these relations may take in the coming years.

Potential for Open Diplomatic Relations

One possibility discussed is the future establishment of open diplomatic relations between Saudi Arabia and Israel. This would involve the formal recognition of each other's sovereignty, the exchange of ambassadors, and the opening of embassies in each other's capitals. Such a step would represent a major shift in the Middle Eastern political landscape and could have wide-ranging implications for the region.

Diplomatic engagement between Saudi Arabia and Israel has

already occurred quietly behind the scenes. In recent years, there have been reports of secret meetings and intelligence cooperation between the two countries, particularly in their shared concerns about Iran's regional ambitions and support for militant groups. These covert interactions have allowed for cooperation without the public scrutiny and potential backlash that formal diplomatic relations would entail.

However, it is important to note that obstacles must be overcome before this becomes a reality. The Arab-Israeli conflict and the unresolved issue of Palestinian statehood remain deeply sensitive topics for the broader Arab and Muslim world. Any move towards open diplomatic relations with Israel would have to be carefully managed to avoid backlash from these constituencies.

Under the leadership of Crown Prince Mohammed bin Salman, Saudi Arabia has been implementing a series of reforms known as Vision 2030, aimed at modernizing and diversifying the economy while promoting social and cultural liberalization. These reforms have been met with mixed responses domestically, with some factions expressing concern over potential compromises to traditional values and religious principles. Consequently, any decision to establish formal relations with Israel would not only have to navigate the sensitivities of the broader Arab and Muslim world but also the domestic political and religious landscape within Saudi Arabia.

Challenges and Obstacles to Closer Ties

Several challenges and obstacles need to be addressed to foster closer ties between Saudi Arabia and Israel.

1. Arab-Israeli Conflict: The ongoing Arab-Israeli conflict is a significant challenge to closer ties. While Saudi Arabia has

taken steps towards supporting a peace process, the resolution of this conflict remains a key sticking point for establishing normalized relations. Saudi Arabia, as a key player in the Arab world, has historically advocated for a just and lasting solution that addresses the aspirations of the Palestinian people, including the establishment of a viable Palestinian state alongside Israel based on internationally recognized borders. Any progress in Saudi-Israeli relations would need to consider the impact on the broader Arab-Israeli peace process carefully.

2. Palestinian Question: The Palestinian question holds immense importance for Saudi Arabia and the broader Arab world. Arab states, including Saudi Arabia, have traditionally advocated for a two-state solution, with East Jerusalem as the capital of a future Palestinian state. Finding a just and viable solution to this long-standing dispute remains a prerequisite for any comprehensive reconciliation between Saudi Arabia and Israel. Therefore, any progress in Saudi-Israeli relations would have to consider the interests and aspirations of the Palestinian people, as well as the concerns of other Arab states.

3. Treatment of Palestinians and Human Rights: Another obstacle to closer ties is the treatment of Palestinians and human rights concerns. Criticism of Israeli policies towards Palestinians, including settlement expansions and restrictions on movement, has been a long-standing point of contention in the Arab world. Saudi Arabia, as a prominent regional player and the custodian of Islam's two holiest sites, bears a particular responsibility to ensure that any steps towards closer relations with Israel are not seen as an endorsement of such policies or a disregard for the broader Arab and Muslim sentiment.

4. Geopolitical Factors: Geopolitical factors such as the role of Iran and its proxies in the region add complexity to the Saudi-Israeli relationship. Both countries view Iran as a significant threat and share concerns over its regional ambitions. This mutual interest in countering Iran's influence provides an incentive for cooperation. However, navigating this issue requires careful consideration, as any public alignment with Israel could exacerbate tensions with Iran and other regional actors that support Tehran.
5. Geopolitical Implications for the Middle East

The potential establishment of open diplomatic relations between Saudi Arabia and Israel would have significant geopolitical implications for the Middle East. It could potentially reshape alliances and power dynamics in the region. The convergence of Saudi and Israeli interests in countering Iran's influence, combating terrorism, and ensuring regional stability could lead to further cooperation on a broader range of issues.

1. Influence on Arab States: Saudi Arabia, the largest Arab economy and home to the birthplace of Islam, has historically played a significant role in shaping Middle Eastern politics. Its warming relations with Israel could influence other Arab states to reconsider their stance towards Israel. Countries like the United Arab Emirates and Bahrain have already taken steps towards normalization, signing the Abraham Accords in 2020. Saudi Arabia's potential alignment with Israel could further incentivize other Arab states to follow suit, potentially leading to a broader regional acceptance of Israel.
2. Regional Realignments: The potential normalization of Saudi-Israeli relations could trigger responses from other regional actors, affecting the delicate balance of power in the region.

Iran, in particular, views Saudi Arabia as a rival and has used the Israeli-Palestinian conflict as a rallying cry against Arab states. Saudi-Israeli cooperation could intensify this rivalry and potentially escalate tensions in the already volatile region. Additionally, countries like Turkey may perceive such a development as a threat to their regional influence and respond accordingly, further complicating the dynamics of the Middle East.
3. Impact on the United States: Any developments in Saudi-Israeli relations would also have implications for the United States' role in the Middle East. Israel has been a long-standing ally of the United States, while Saudi Arabia has enjoyed a strategic partnership with Washington. The convergence of interests between Saudi Arabia and Israel could strengthen the already close ties between these countries and the United States, potentially leading to a realignment of alliances and shaping the dynamics of the broader region.

In conclusion, the future prospects for Saudi-Israeli relations are both promising and challenging. While there is potential for open diplomatic relations, various obstacles and sensitivities must be navigated. The impact of these relations on the broader Middle East cannot be underestimated, and it will require careful diplomacy, strategic thinking, and a nuanced understanding of regional dynamics to shape a future that promotes stability, security, and cooperation.

A. POTENTIAL FOR OPEN DIPLOMATIC RELATIONS

Saudi Arabia and Israel

In recent years, there have been growing speculations about the potential for open diplomatic relations between Saudi Arabia and Israel. While the two countries have long been at odds due to historical and geopolitical reasons, several factors have emerged that suggest the possibility of a significant shift in their relationship.

One key factor contributing to the potential for open diplomatic relations is the shared concern over Iran's regional ambitions. Both Saudi Arabia and Israel view Iran as a major threat due to its support for proxy groups, such as Hezbollah and Hamas, and its pursuit of nuclear capabilities. This common enemy has led to behind-the-scenes cooperation and intelligence sharing between the two countries in order to counter Iran's influence. The United States, a major ally for both Saudi Arabia and Israel, has also been increasingly vocal about Iran's destabilizing activities in the region. The U.S. withdrawal from the Iran nuclear deal in 2018 and the reimposition of sanctions further intensified the need for coordination between these nations. Recognizing the need for a united front against Iran, Saudi Arabia has been more open to exploring avenues of cooperation with Israel, given their shared security concerns.

Under Crown Prince Mohammad bin Salman's Vision 2030 plan, Saudi Arabia's leadership aims to transform the country's economy and reduce its reliance on oil. In this context, forging closer ties with Israel, a prominent technological and innovation hub, could offer Saudi Arabia access to advanced technologies in sectors such as agriculture, water management, and renewable energy. Israel's expertise in these areas, coupled with its robust start-up ecosystem, presents attractive opportunities for Saudi Arabia to diversify its economy and achieve its ambitious goals. Economic engagement between the two countries could lead to significant mutual benefits, boosting trade, investment opportunities, and job creation.

Another factor driving the potential for diplomatic relations is the changing dynamics of the Middle East. The Arab-Israeli conflict, which has long been a major obstacle to normalization, has lost some of its prominence in recent years. Many Arab nations have shifted their focus towards more pressing issues like terrorism, stability, and economic development. The historic Abraham Accords signed in 2020 between Israel, the United Arab Emirates, and Bahrain marked a significant turning point, as they set a precedent for Arab nations openly normalizing their relations with Israel. The normalization between these Arab states and Israel has created a more conducive environment for Saudi Arabia to consider open engagement. The potential for increased regional cooperation, trade, and tourism resulting from these accords provides an incentive for Saudi Arabia to adjust its stance.

Furthermore, the evolving regional power dynamics, with the emergence of new actors and the changing priorities of established powers, have created opportunities for a reevaluation of Saudi-Israeli relations. The rise of non-state actors such as the Islamic State (IS) and other extremist groups has destabilized the region and heightened concerns about security and stability. Saudi Arabia and Israel, being strong regional powers, have a shared interest in countering these extremist threats. Additionally, the shifting stance of global powers, such as the United States, towards a more realpolitik approach in the region has influenced the Saudis to consider the potential benefits of closer cooperation with Israel. The U.S., under the Trump administration, openly supported the Abraham Accords and encouraged other Arab nations to follow suit, signaling a change in the traditional diplomatic approach towards Israel.

However, some significant challenges and obstacles need to be addressed for open diplomatic relations to become a reality. One major hurdle is the long-standing Palestinian issue. Saudi Arabia, as a prominent Muslim nation and a guardian of the Islamic holy sites, has historically championed the cause of the Palestinians. King Salman, the custodian of the two holy mosques, has consistently emphasized the importance of finding a just and lasting solution for the Palestinian people. Any normalization of relations with Israel would require careful consideration of the impact on the Palestinian cause and finding a solution that is acceptable to both parties. Saudi Arabia has openly expressed that any potential normalization would be contingent on the establishment of an independent Palestinian state based on pre-1967 borders and with East Jerusalem as its capital. Saudi Arabia's commitment to the Palestinian cause has been further reinforced by its financial support to the Palestinian Authority and its efforts to unite Palestinian factions for a cohesive approach to negotiations.

Additionally, there are domestic concerns within Saudi Arabia that may resist moves towards closer engagement with Israel. The conservative religious establishment, which plays a significant role in shaping public opinion and societal norms, has historically been opposed to the normalization of relations with Israel. This conservative wing fears that normalizing relations could undermine the Palestinian cause and compromise the sanctity of Islamic holy sites. The influence of the religious leaders cannot be underestimated, and any diplomatic strides towards Israel would require careful consideration and navigational strategies to address these concerns.

Public opinion also plays a crucial role in determining the approach taken by the Saudi government. While there has been a notable shift in attitudes towards Israel among some segments of the Saudi population, fueled by increased exposure to Israeli culture, technology, and economic success, there is still a significant portion that holds anti-israel solid sentiment. Managing and shaping public opinion will be a key aspect of any potential diplomatic engagement. The Saudi leadership will need to educate the public about the potential benefits of normalization, address concerns and misconceptions, and foster understanding between the two nations to gain public support.

In conclusion, the potential for open diplomatic relations between Saudi Arabia and Israel is a topic of growing interest and speculation. While several factors contribute to this potential, such as shared regional concerns and changing dynamics in the Middle East, significant challenges and obstacles remain. The resolution of the Palestinian issue and managing domestic sensitivities are among the key considerations. The future of Saudi-Israeli relations will depend on carefully navigating these complexities, with potential implications for the broader Middle Eastern dynamics and the global geopolitical landscape. As the regional and international contexts shift, it is essential to closely monitor the evolving dynamics and the geopolitical calculations of the key actors involved.

B. CHALLENGES AND OBSTACLES TO CLOSER TIES

Developing closer ties between Saudi Arabia and Israel has challenges and obstacles. While there has been progress in recent years, several key factors continue to impede the establishment of full-fledged diplomatic relations and deeper cooperation. This chapter will explore these challenges and the potential obstacles to a stronger Saudi-Israeli relationship.

1. Historical Context: The historical context of conflict and animosity between Arabs and Israelis has spanned several decades and is a significant barrier to closer ties. The Arab-Israeli wars, including the 1948 war, the Six-Day War in 1967, and the Yom Kippur War in 1973, have been defining moments in the relationship. These conflicts not only

resulted in territorial disputes but also led to significant loss of life and displacement of Palestinians. These historical events have shaped public sentiment in Saudi Arabia, influencing the overall anti-Israeli sentiment that persists today.
2. Palestinian Question: The Israeli-Palestinian conflict remains a significant obstacle in Saudi-Israeli relations. Saudi Arabia has historically been a vocal supporter of Palestinian rights and the establishment of an independent Palestinian state with East Jerusalem as its capital. The Saudi government's commitment to the Palestinian cause is deeply ingrained in its society, making it politically challenging for the government to openly embrace Israel without adequately addressing this issue.

Efforts towards peace, such as the Oslo Accords signed in the 1990s and subsequent negotiations, have failed to resolve the conflict, leading to frustration and disillusionment among Palestinians and many in the Arab world. As a result, Saudi Arabia's stance on the Palestinian question has remained central to its foreign policy, shaping its approach to relations with Israel.

1. Religious and Cultural Differences: Religious and cultural differences between Saudi Arabia and Israel pose another challenge to closer ties. Saudi Arabia follows a strict interpretation of Sunni Islam, while Israel is a predominantly Jewish state. These religious and cultural disparities can create barriers to closer understanding and cooperation. Additionally, antagonism towards Israel is deeply rooted in the Muslim world, making it difficult for Saudi Arabia to normalize relations without facing significant backlash from its own population and other Muslim-majority countries.
2. Geopolitical Considerations: Saudi Arabia must navigate its

alliances with other Arab countries in the region, many of which do not have formal ties with Israel. Aligning closely with Israel could strain existing alliances and potentially impact regional stability. The Arab Peace Initiative, put forward by Saudi Arabia in 2002, offered normalization with Israel by multiple Arab states in exchange for a complete withdrawal from occupied territories and a just resolution to the Palestinian refugee issue. While there has been limited progress in recent years, the fear of undermining regional unity remains a significant geopolitical challenge.

Further complicating the Saudi-Israeli relationship is Iran's regional influence and its antagonistic stance towards both Saudi Arabia and Israel. Iran's support for various groups, such as Hezbollah and Hamas, who oppose both countries, creates a regional power struggle and adds another layer of complexity to Saudi-Israeli relations.

1. Domestic Politics and Leadership Dynamics: Changes in leadership within Saudi Arabia and Israel can affect the trajectory of their relationship. Political stability and continuity of leadership are critical for developing long-term cooperation. Domestic politics within each country, including public opinion, interest groups, and domestic policy priorities, also significantly shape the relationship. Public sentiment in Saudi Arabia towards Israel, influenced by the Israeli-Palestinian conflict, represents a challenge for the government as it tries to balance national interests and public opinion.

In Israel, the coalition governments formed through complex negotiations between various political parties can impact the country's approach to relations with Saudi Arabia. The need for consensus among stakeholders within each country adds another layer of complexity to the relationship and requires careful navigation.

1. Economic Challenges: The economic ties between Saudi Arabia and Israel are still limited. Opening trade relations and developing economic cooperation face significant hurdles, including competition from other regional and global economic partners. Economic diversification efforts within Saudi Arabia, such as Vision 2030, aim to reduce the country's dependence on oil and promote a knowledge-based economy. While this offers potential avenues for collaboration, it also requires time, investment, and structural changes for both countries to benefit from greater economic integration fully.

Overcoming these challenges and obstacles will require more than diplomatic finesse, visionary leadership, and sustained efforts from both Saudi Arabia and Israel. Continuous dialogue, trust-building measures, and addressing the concerns of each side are not enough to foster greater understanding and cooperation. Only regional and international mediation efforts for an actual peace deal in Palestine can facilitate progress and mitigate potential risks. Only recognising an independent Palestinian State is the foundation for regional stability, security, and economic progress, making pursuing stronger relations worthwhile and necessary in today's ever-changing geopolitical landscape.

C. GEOPOLITICAL IMPLICATIONS FOR THE MIDDLE EAST

The evolving relationship between Saudi Arabia and Israel has significant geopolitical implications for the Middle East. These implications extend beyond bilateral ties and have far-reaching consequences for regional dynamics and power struggles.

Firstly, the establishment of overt diplomatic relations between Saudi Arabia and Israel would be a monumental shift in the Middle Eastern geopolitical landscape only after the recognition of an independent Palestinian state, not before. The region has been characterized by a deep-rooted animosity towards Israel since its establishment in 1948, with Arab nations viewing it as an occupier of Palestinian territories. The Arab-Israeli conflict, marked by multiple wars and ongoing tensions, has shaped regional politics for decades. A diplomatic breakthrough between Saudi Arabia and Israel, if based on mutual respect for the Palestinian rights, could benefit the region.

The US-Israeli belief is that the potential normalization of relations between Saudi Arabia and Israel would not only affect bilateral ties but also reshape alliances and influence other countries' stances towards Israel. While several Arab states, notably Egypt and Jordan, have already established diplomatic relations with Israel, Saudi recognition would carry significant weight due to its role as the custodian of Islam's holiest sites in Mecca and Medina. Other Arab countries, who have long followed Saudi Arabia's lead on regional affairs, might follow suit, reassessing their policy towards Israel and potentially looking to forge diplomatic ties as well. This potential ripple effect could reshape the region's political landscape and redefine alliances that have persisted for years. That would be true only if the Palestinian people regained independence and sovereignty on its land.

Secondly, Saudi-Israeli cooperation in countering Iranian influence has the potential to reshape the balance of power in the Middle East. Both nations view Iran as a common regional threat due to its pursuit of nuclear weapons, destabilizing activities, and support for proxy militias across the region. This is no longer true, given the Chinese mediation that resulted in a reconciliation between Iran and the KSA.

The USA thinks that closer cooperation between Saudi Arabia and Israel allows for increased intelligence sharing, joint military exercises, and coordinated strategies to counter Iran's regional ambitions. This alignment of interests could significantly impact regional dynamics and Saudi Arabia's position as a leader in the Arab world. But is Iran the enemy of Saudi Arabia or the enemy of Israel and the USA? The confusion is easy and the Saudi leaders have been trapped into it for decades. Today, they seem to have second thoughts.

Furthermore, the Saudi-Israeli relationship has implications for ongoing regional conflicts, notably the Arab-Israeli conflict and the broader Israeli-Palestinian issue. According to the US view, the prospect of Saudi Arabia recognizing Israel could signal a significant shift in the broader Arab stance towards Israel, potentially encouraging other Arab nations to reconsider their approach. They omit to say it could also trigger a general revolt in Muslim majority countries against the Saudi regime and also inside the kingdom.

Only Israel's readiness for the recognition of an independent Palestinian state could provide a fresh impetus for peace negotiations and a possible resolution to the Israeli-Palestinian conflict. Saudi Arabia's influence and financial resources could also play a vital role in supporting Palestinian state-building efforts and facilitating peace talks.

In addition to the Arab-Israeli conflict, the Saudi-Israeli relationship influences other regional struggles, such as the Yemeni Civil War and the Syrian conflict. Cooperation between Saudi Arabia and Israel, after recognition of a Free Palestine, could lead to joint efforts in resolving all other conflicts. With their respective political, military, and economic influence, both countries could work towards stabilizing the region and finding political solutions. But right now, such cooperation would appear sinful to millions of people, because of the Palestinian plight. It is crucial to consider the potential opposition from other regional players who may perceive this cooperation as a threat to their interests, particularly Iran, which has significant influence in both Yemen and Syria through its proxies.

Moreover, the geopolitical implications of the assumed Saudi-Israeli relations extend beyond the Middle East itself and warrant the attention of major global powers. The United States, for instance, has traditionally been a crucial ally to both Saudi Arabia and Israel (actually more to Israel than to Saudi Arabia). Closer ties between Saudi Arabia and Israel could provide an opportunity for the U.S. to further its interests in the region and reshape its approach to the broader Middle East. In recent years, the U.S. has actively sought to foster closer ties between Arab nations and Israel as part of its broader strategy for stability and cooperation in the region. However, it failed to advance the peace agenda in Palestine and gave Israel a free hand in the genocide in Gaza.

The extended Saudi-Israeli relationship could also have an impact on global energy markets. Saudi Arabia, as the world's largest oil exporter, and Israel, with its burgeoning natural gas industry, possess substantial energy resources and strategic transportation routes. Closer collaboration in the energy sector could lead to joint ventures, regional pipelines, and enhanced energy security for both countries. This cooperation could also draw the attention of other major energy players, such as Russia and China, who may seek to strengthen their own ties and influence in the region. The only problem is the Palestinian issue.

Furthermore, the Saudi-Israeli relationship holds significant implications for religious dynamics in the Middle East. As we said, if revealed, it can trigger a revolt inside the kingdom and in the broader Muslim world. Who would go to pilgrimage under the Israeli flag?

The recognition of Israel by Saudi Arabia, a country that carries great religious authority as the guardian of the Islamic holy sites, could potentially prompt changes in the attitudes of Islamic scholars and Muslims worldwide towards the Kingdom of Saudi Arabia. This could have far-reaching effects regionally and internationally.

The Saudi-Israeli collaboration in technology, cybersecurity, and innovation brings new possibilities for both countries to propel their economies and contribute to technological advancements in the region. Joint research initiatives, startup incubators, and knowledge-sharing can foster an environment of scientific and technological progress, benefitting both nations and the broader Middle Eastern region. Again, it is a secret relationship that would upset the Muslims of the world if revealed while thousands of people in Palestine are still under occupation and victims of genocide.

The secret Saudi-Israeli relationship also necessitates carefully managing potential challenges and risks. The historical complexities of the Arab-Israeli conflict, deeply rooted regional rivalries, internal domestic pressures, and differing strategic priorities all pose significant challenges to sustaining and deepening this relationship. It would require diplomatic finesse, visionary leadership, and skillful navigations to overcome such obstacles and realize the full potential of this dynamic shift in Middle Eastern geopolitics.

In conclusion, the geopolitical implications of the Saudi-Israeli relationship in the Middle East are multifaceted. The potential establishment of diplomatic relations, regional cooperation against common threats, influence on ongoing conflicts, impact on global diplomacy, energy markets, religious dynamics, and technological advancements all would contribute to a new geopolitical landscape in the region at the condition that Palestine is free. As these secret relationships continue to evolve, the world will closely monitor the outcomes and adjustments required to accommodate this shifting Middle Eastern geopolitical terrain. It would be either stability after recognition of an independent Palestine, or the tempest.

In a Nutshell

A. Potential for Open Diplomatic Relations

The potential for open diplomatic relations between Saudi Arabia and Israel by 2030 is cautiously optimistic. Recent developments suggest a growing momentum towards normalization, influenced by strategic interests and external pressures. The U.S. and Saudi Arabia have agreed on the broad contours of a deal for Saudi Arabia to recognize Israel, which includes concessions to the Palestinians, U.S. security guarantees, and civilian nuclear assistance. This agreement aligns with Saudi Arabia's Vision 2030, which aims to diversify its economy and reduce its oil dependency, potentially benefiting from Israeli technological and economic collaboration.

Furthermore, the changing political landscape in Saudi Arabia, particularly with the anticipated transition in leadership from King Salman to Crown Prince Mohammed bin Salman, could facilitate a more decisive approach towards normalization. The Crown Prince has shown a pragmatic stance towards Israel, recognizing the strategic benefits of such a relationship in countering mutual threats like Iran and leveraging U.S. support.

B. Challenges and Obstacles to Closer Ties

Despite the potential for diplomatic breakthroughs, several challenges and obstacles could impede closer ties between Saudi Arabia and Israel. The Palestinian issue remains a significant barrier. Saudi Arabia has consistently emphasized that the establishment of a Palestinian state is a precondition for normalization. The current Israeli government's reluctance to make substantial concessions to the Palestinians complicates this requirement.

Additionally, domestic and regional political dynamics pose challenges. The Saudi public and broader Muslim world hold deep-seated views on the Palestinian cause, and any move towards normalization without addressing these concerns could lead to internal and external backlash. Moreover, the recent détente between Saudi Arabia and Iran, brokered by China, introduces a new variable that could either detract from or add complexity to Saudi-Israeli relations, depending on how regional alignments shift.

C. Geopolitical Implications for the Middle East

The normalization of relations between Saudi Arabia and Israel would have profound geopolitical implications for the Middle East. It could significantly alter the regional power dynamics, positioning Saudi Arabia and Israel as central players in a new Middle Eastern order. This alignment could lead to a more robust front against common adversaries like Iran, potentially stabilizing the region or escalating tensions depending on the reactions from Tehran and its proxies.

Furthermore, a Saudi-Israeli rapprochement could influence

other Arab states' policies towards Israel and potentially lead to broader regional normalization, building on the foundation of the Abraham Accords. This shift could also affect the influence of global powers in the Middle East, with the United States seeking to maintain its strategic interests while China and Russia could look to expand their influence amidst changing alliances.

In conclusion, the trajectory towards open diplomatic relations between Saudi Arabia and Israel by 2030 is marked by both promising opportunities and significant challenges. While strategic interests and potential leadership changes in Saudi Arabia suggest a favorable outlook, the complexities of the Palestinian issue and regional geopolitics will play critical roles in shaping the future of this pivotal relationship.

Sources and References

[1] https://www.mei.edu/publications/oncoming-saudi-israeli-normalization-obstacles-opportunities-and-us-role

[2] https://www.nytimes.com/2023/10/08/us/politics/saudi-arabia-israel-palestinians-hamas.html

[3] https://www.cnbc.com/2023/09/01/saudi-arabia-israel-deal-could-dramatically-reshape-the-middle-east-.html

[4] https://www.newsweek.com/biden-wasting-his-time-israel-saudi-normalization-deal-opinion-1886686

[5] https://www.brookings.edu/articles/the-new-geopolitics-of-the-middle-east-americas-role-in-a-changing-region/

[6] https://www.washingtonpost.com/world/2023/09/21/saudi-israel-normalization-biden-netanyahu/

[7] https://www.atlanticcouncil.org/blogs/menasource/saudi-arabia-israel-two-state-gaza-normalization/

[8] https://www.bloomberg.com/news/articles/2023-09-22/a-saudi-israeli-peace-deal-who-wants-what-and-why

[9] https://carnegieendowment.org/2020/10/15/what-would-happen-if-israel-and-saudi-arabia-established-official-relations-pub-82964

[10] https://world101.cfr.org/rotw/middle-east/geopolitics

[11] https://www.hoover.org/research/will-saudi-arabia-normalize-relations-israel

[12] https://www.dw.com/en/will-the-hamas-israel-conflict-derail-saudi-arabias-ambitious-plans-for-its-future/a-67223432

[13] https://www.orsam.org.tr/en/from-regional-isolation-to-engagement-exploring-the-prospects-of-saudi-israel-normalization/

[14] https://www.theguardian.com/world/2023/sep/21/saudi-arabia-getting-closer-to-normalising-relations-with-israel-crown-prince-says

[15] https://www.fairobserver.com/politics/arab-world/tentative-steps-toward-a-new-saudi-israeli-relationship/

[16] https://edition.cnn.com/2023/08/14/middleeast/saudi-appoints-first-envoy-palestinians-intl/index.html

[17] https://www.usip.org/publications/2023/09/saudi-israel-normalization-agreement-horizon

[18] https://www.dailysabah.com/business/economy/saudi-arabia-warns-of-economic-fallout-from-gaza-war-geopolitics

[19] https://www.brookings.edu/articles/israel-in-the-middle-east-the-next-two-decades/

VIII

Implications for Global Diplomacy

Saudi-Israeli relations have significant implications for global diplomacy. As these two nations have historically been at odds, any shifts or advancements in their relationship can have reverberating effects on the international stage. The evolving Saudi-Israeli relationship has the potential to reshape existing global alliances. It requires careful navigation for all involved parties, posing challenges and opportunities for various countries worldwide.

Saudi-Israeli Relations and Global Alliances

The evolving relationship between Saudi Arabia and Israel has the potential to reshape global alliances, particularly for countries directly involved in the Middle East. Traditionally, Saudi Arabia has been a key ally to the United States, forming the bedrock of the strategic partnership in the region. The Kingdom's influence has extended to other countries in the Gulf Cooperation Council

(GCC), strengthening the alignment with the West. This alliance has been crucial for maintaining regional stability and ensuring the flow of oil, a vital global resource.

However, the warming ties between Saudi Arabia and Israel – contrasting with the regional tensions - create a complex dynamic that requires careful navigation. On the one hand, enhanced cooperation between these two countries may present an opportunity for broader regional stability in the US's eyes. Mutual recognition and the pursuit of common interests, such as countering Iran's influence, combating terrorism, and promoting economic development, could contribute to a more secure and prosperous Middle East, according to the US view.

On the other hand, this evolving alliance could strain established relationships and create tensions within existing global alliances. The United States and other Western powers have historically had to balance their relationships with both Saudi Arabia and Israel, often finding themselves caught in the middle of conflicting interests or perspectives. This balancing act poses a challenge for global diplomacy, as these nations must carefully manage their relationships with multiple actors in the region, considering their own strategic interests and obligations.

International Reactions and Diplomatic Considerations

The rapprochement between Saudi Arabia and Israel has elicited mixed reactions from the international community. While Western nations have welcomed the potential for enhanced regional stability resulting from improved Saudi-Israeli relations, others view it with caution and skepticism.

Countries within the Arab and Muslim worlds, especially those with a history of supporting the Palestinian cause, may perceive the warming ties as a betrayal of Arab solidarity. The Palestinian issue remains a complex and deeply rooted conflict, and any progress towards normalization between Saudi Arabia and Israel might be seen as undermining efforts to find a just and lasting solution. Diplomatic efforts must address these concerns by emphasizing the importance of a comprehensive and inclusive peace process that addresses the legitimate aspirations of the Palestinian people.

On the other hand, countries with historically close relations with Israel might have to navigate the challenges of dealing with a key Arab ally having significant interactions with their long-standing partner. These nations must strike a delicate balance between maintaining their relationships with both Saudi Arabia and Israel while ensuring that their actions contribute to stability in the region.

For global diplomacy, managing these varied reactions and promoting understanding among nations with divergent viewpoints is crucial. Engaging in dialogue and fostering diplomacy can help address concerns and build bridges of understanding. Multilateral forums, such as the United Nations and regional organizations like the Arab League and Organization of Islamic Cooperation, can serve as vital platforms for discussion and collaboration while recognizing the complexities and sensitivities involved.

The Role of Other Global Powers

The evolving Saudi-Israeli relationship also requires other global powers to reassess their strategies and roles in the Middle East. Non-regional actors, such as Russia and China, have been expanding their influence in the region and keenly observing the changing dynamics between Saudi Arabia and Israel.

Russia, for instance, has been seeking to assert itself as a significant player in regional conflicts, such as the Syrian civil war. The evolving Saudi-Israeli relationship may impact Russia's engagement in the region. With longstanding ties to Syria and Iran, Russia must consider the implications of improved Saudi-Israeli relations on its own interests and influence. It may seek to leverage its relationships with both countries to play a constructive role in mediating conflicts and ensuring regional stability.

Similarly, China's increasing economic ties and infrastructure initiatives in the Middle East, such as the Belt and Road Initiative, have positioned it as an emerging player in the region. As China seeks to maintain stability and secure its economic interests, it will need to manage the evolving dynamics between Saudi Arabia and Israel carefully. Balancing its relationships with both countries, China must exercise caution to avoid being drawn into regional conflicts or exacerbating tensions. Its diplomatic approach should prioritize stability, economic cooperation, and non-interference in internal affairs.

The implications for global diplomacy, therefore, go beyond traditional Western powers. As the relationship between Saudi Arabia and Israel continues to develop, diplomats and policymakers need to consider other global powers' varied reactions and interests and engage in constructive dialogue to promote peace, stability, and mutual understanding in the broader global context.

In conclusion, the implications for global diplomacy resulting from the evolving Saudi-Israeli relationship are multifaceted and require careful navigation. The potential restructuring of existing alliances, the varied international reactions, and the impact on other global powers necessitate comprehensive analysis and strategic decision-making. By engaging in constructive diplomacy, leveraging multilateral platforms, and considering the interests of all parties involved, global diplomats and policymakers can contribute to fostering peace, stability, and cooperation in the Middle East and beyond. This complex process demands sensitivity, pragmatism, and a determination to find common ground amidst diverse perspectives and interests.

A. SAUDI-ISRAELI RELATIONS AND GLOBAL ALLIANCES

Saudi-Israeli relations have long been a subject of interest and speculation given the historical context of the Middle East. In this chapter, we delve into the implications of these relations on global alliances and the broader international community.

The intersection of Saudi Arabia and Israel on the global stage raises several important questions. How do their ties with other international powers factor into their bilateral relations? What are the implications for global diplomacy and regional stability? We examine the dynamics between Saudi Arabia, Israel, and other major global players to explore these questions.

Both Saudi Arabia and Israel have historically relied on strong alliances with global powers to navigate the complex geopolitical landscape of the Middle East. Saudi Arabia, being a key oil exporter and a significant player in the Arab world, has established close ties with numerous countries across the globe. It has maintained long-standing alliances with the United States and European powers, which have helped secure its regional interests.

The United States has played a particularly vital role in Saudi Arabia's global alliances. The strong partnership between the two countries is built on mutual economic and strategic interests. The United States relies on Saudi Arabia for its oil reserves and military cooperation. In return, Saudi Arabia benefits from American military protection, access to advanced weaponry, and economic investments. This alliance has shaped the balance of power in the Middle East and has been influential in global oil markets and energy security.

Similarly, Israel has relied heavily on its relationship with the United States as its primary ally. The U.S.-Israel alliance has been crucial in shaping the political, military, and economic landscape of the region. The United States has consistently supported Israel diplomatically and financially, providing substantial military aid and access to advanced military technologies. This alliance has also garnered significant support from other nations, largely due to historical connections, shared values, and geopolitical considerations.

The Saudi-Israeli relationship impacts these global alliances in various ways. Firstly, it introduces an element of complexity in the already intricate Middle Eastern dynamics. Saudi Arabia's evolving relationship with Israel may influence its interactions and alignments with other countries in the region, particularly those that take a more antagonistic stance towards Israel.

For instance, Saudi Arabia's recent steps towards rapprochement with Israel have led to a significant shift in regional dynamics. The Gulf states, such as the United Arab Emirates and Bahrain, have followed suit and established official diplomatic relations with Israel. This alignment of Arab nations that were previously opposed to recognizing Israel has potentially reshaped traditional regional alliances and is influencing other Arab countries to reassess their positions.

Additionally, Saudi-Israeli relations have broader ripple effects on global alliances, including those beyond the Middle East. As Saudi Arabia becomes more willing to engage with Israel, traditional allies may need to reevaluate their positions and adjust their policies accordingly. This could potentially lead to shifts in global power dynamics and realignments among major players in the international community.

China, for example, has been growing its influence in the Middle East through economic investments and partnerships. As Saudi Arabia and Israel strengthen their ties, China may find itself navigating a more complex landscape, where its relationships with both countries need careful management. A similar scenario may unfold for countries like Russia and India, both of which have emerged as important players in the region and have their own geopolitical interests to balance.

Furthermore, the implications of Saudi-Israeli relations on the Israeli-Palestinian conflict play a significant role in global alliances. The Israeli-Palestinian issue has long been a core concern for many nations, and any developments in Saudi-Israeli relations can impact the international community's approach to this longstanding conflict. Global alliances that have traditionally supported the Palestinian cause may need to navigate their relationships and policies in light of evolving dynamics in the Middle East.

The shifting Saudi stance towards Israel has created both challenges and opportunities for international efforts to resolve the Israeli-Palestinian conflict. Countries supporting a two-state solution, such as European nations and the United Nations, may need to adapt their strategies and engage with regional actors in new ways. Conversely, countries like Iran and Turkey, which have been critical of Saudi-Israeli relations, may find themselves strengthening their existing alliances to counterbalance the evolving dynamics in the region.

Moreover, the growing relationship between Saudi Arabia and Israel has implications for regional security and stability. Cooperation between the two countries in intelligence-sharing, counter-terrorism efforts, and military cooperation can have lasting effects on the balance of power in the Middle East. This may lead to re-evaluating regional alliances, especially among Arab states, as they seek to navigate the evolving landscape.

The evolving Saudi-Israeli relationship also presents opportunities for economic cooperation and integration. Both countries have advanced economies, technological capabilities, and investment potential. Strengthening ties through trade agreements, investment partnerships, and technological collaboration can unlock significant economic opportunities for Saudi Arabia and Israel and their global allies.

Ultimately, the interplay between Saudi-Israeli relations and global alliances underscores the complexity of the Middle East and the broader international landscape. These relations have the potential to reshape existing power dynamics, realign global alliances, have implications on regional security, and impact ongoing conflicts in the region. As Saudi Arabia and Israel continue to navigate their relationship within the global context, policymakers and analysts must closely monitor and understand the implications for regional stability, global diplomacy, economic integration, and efforts towards conflict resolution.

B. INTERNATIONAL REACTIONS AND DIPLOMATIC CONSIDERATIONS

The dynamic between Saudi Arabia and Israel has far-reaching implications for the international community. As Saudi-Israeli relations continue to develop and potentially evolve towards open diplomatic ties, it is crucial to analyze the reactions and considerations of other countries and international entities.

One of the most significant reactions to the Saudi-Israeli

Saudi Arabia and Israel

relationship comes from the broader Arab and Muslim world. Historically, these regions have been staunch supporters of Palestinian rights and have viewed Israel as an occupying force. The potential normalization of relations between Saudi Arabia and Israel could lead to mixed reactions from Arab and Muslim countries.

Some states may view this development as a betrayal of the Palestinian cause, while others may cautiously welcome it as a step towards stability and a more balanced approach to regional issues. Within the Arab world, there is a spectrum of viewpoints, ranging from those who prioritize solidarity with Palestinians to those who prioritize strategic alliances and regional stability. Various factors, including historical ties with Israel, political considerations, and the specific ideological leaning of each country will influence the response to the evolving Saudi-Israeli relationship.

For countries that have historically maintained a more aggressive position towards Israel, such as Iran, Syria, and Lebanon, the potential normalization of relations between Saudi Arabia and Israel poses a significant challenge. These countries have been at odds with Israel for decades for both geopolitical and ideological reasons. Iran, in particular, has positioned itself as the standard-bearer of Palestinian rights and has been a vocal opponent of Israeli policies. Any strengthening of ties between Saudi Arabia and Israel could challenge Iran's regional ambitions and potentially escalate existing rivalries.

Turkey, another regional power, has traditionally supported the Palestinian cause and has been highly critical of Israeli policies towards Palestinians. Turkish President Recep Tayyip Erdogan has been vocal in his condemnation of Israel, often using inflammatory rhetoric. The potential rapprochement between Saudi Arabia and Israel could further complicate Turkey's regional ambitions and lead to a divergence in Turkish-Arab relations.

Qatar, a key player in the region, has previously supported the

Palestinian cause but has also maintained diplomatic channels with Israel. As a mediator and a financier of various projects in the Middle East, Qatar has walked a delicate diplomatic tightrope. The evolving relationship between Saudi Arabia and Israel could impact Qatar's position and its ability to navigate regional dynamics without alienating key stakeholders.

The United States and other Western powers play a pivotal role in broader international diplomacy. The United States has been a long-standing ally of Israel and has been actively involved in brokering peace agreements in the region. The reaction of the United States to the evolving Saudi-Israeli relationship will profoundly shape its trajectory.

Under different administrations, US policy towards the Middle East has varied. While some US administrations might embrace closer ties between Saudi Arabia and Israel, others might be more cautious, considering the implications for regional stability and the potential impact on other alliances, such as the US relationship with Iran or other Arab states. Additionally, the US response will likely be influenced by domestic politics, including the influence of pro-Israel lobbying groups and the opinions of the American Jewish community.

Furthermore, European countries, particularly those involved in the Middle East peace process, will closely watch the developments between Saudi Arabia and Israel. These countries have historically supported a two-state solution and have played a significant role in diplomatic efforts aimed at resolving the Israeli-Palestinian conflict. They have a vested interest in the stability of the region and ensuring that any progress in Saudi-Israeli relations considers the rights and aspirations of the Palestinian people. The reactions of these countries will depend on their own geopolitical interests and their assessments of the Saudi-Israeli relationship's impact on the broader region.

Russia, another significant player in the region, has been expanding its influence in the Middle East in recent years. While Russia has historically maintained good relations with Arab countries, it has also developed diplomatic ties with Israel. Moscow has positioned itself as a mediator in the Israeli-Palestinian conflict and has hosted peace talks in the past. As Saudi Arabia and Israel potentially move closer, Russia's response will be crucial in determining its role in ongoing diplomatic efforts.

It is also important to consider the positions of international organizations, such as the United Nations (UN) and the Arab League. The UN has been actively involved in peace negotiations and has passed numerous resolutions related to the Israeli-Palestinian conflict. Its response to the evolving Saudi-Israeli relationship will depend on its commitment to a two-state solution and the preservation of Palestinian rights. As a multilateral organization, the UN will face the challenge of accommodating its member states' diverse opinions and interests while continuing to advocate for a just resolution to the Israeli-Palestinian conflict.

The Arab League, a regional organization comprising predominantly Arab states, has traditionally been a vocal supporter of the Palestinian cause and has remained critical of Israel's actions. The league's response to the evolving Saudi-Israeli relationship will depend on the extent to which Saudi Arabia's position influences the collective stance of its member states. Other factors, such as political dynamics and historical alliances within the Arab League, could shape its response, potentially leading to divisions among member states.

In conclusion, the international reactions and diplomatic considerations surrounding the Saudi-Israeli relationship are complex and multifaceted. The responses of other countries, regional powers, and international organizations will likely be shaped by their strategic interests, historical alliances, and geopolitical calculations.

Understanding these reactions is crucial for comprehending the broader implications of the developing Saudi-Israeli relationship on regional stability and global diplomacy. The interplay between these actors will shape the future trajectory of the Saudi-Israeli relationship and its impact on the broader Middle East region.

C. THE ROLE OF OTHER GLOBAL POWERS

Throughout the complex Saudi-Israeli relationship, other global powers have played a significant and multifaceted role, shaping the dynamics and influencing the trajectory of their interactions. These powers, including the United States, Russia, China, and European Union countries, cannot be overlooked when analyzing the broader implications of Saudi-Israeli relations.

The United States has historically been a key player in shaping the Middle East's geopolitical landscape. Its strategic alliance with Saudi Arabia, rooted in shared security interests, has had a profound impact on the Saudi-Israeli relationship. The United States has positioned itself as a mediator between the two countries, leveraging its influence to defuse tensions and encourage dialogue. Throughout the years, the U.S. has played a crucial role in brokering peace agreements such as the Camp David Accords in 1978 and the Oslo Accords in 1993. By facilitating direct talks and offering incentives, the U.S. has worked to bridge the gaps and facilitate common ground between Saudi Arabia and Israel. Additionally, Washington's military and economic aid to Saudi Arabia and Israel has provided both countries with the necessary resources to navigate regional challenges effectively. The United States' involvement

Saudi Arabia and Israel

in the region continues to influence the nature and progress of the Saudi-Israeli relationship.

Russia, another major global power, has actively sought to exert its influence in the Middle East, including in the context of Saudi-Israeli relations. As a historical ally of Arab nations, Russia has had a complicated relationship with Israel. However, over the past decade, it has taken steps towards forging closer ties with Israel, acknowledging its importance as a regional power. This recalibration has been driven by Russia's geopolitical ambitions and economic interests. Seeking to expand its influence beyond its traditional sphere of influence, Russia has cultivated closer ties with Saudi Arabia, particularly in terms of energy cooperation and military partnerships. Russia has played a role in brokering the Astana peace process for Syria, where it has hosted talks between Saudi Arabian-backed opposition groups and the Syrian government, indirectly influencing dynamics in the region. By maintaining a delicate balance between its relationships with Saudi Arabia and Israel, Russia manages to play a constructive role in the Saudi-Israeli dynamic, continuing to shape the region's geopolitical landscape.

China, with its growing global influence, has also made its mark on the Middle East and entered the scene of Saudi-Israeli relations. China's increasing energy needs have led to closer economic ties with Saudi Arabia, making it an essential trading partner for the kingdom. These economic interests have been further solidified through initiatives such as China's Belt and Road Initiative, which seeks to strengthen infrastructure and connectivity with the region. This closer economic engagement has extended to investments in infrastructure projects and the promotion of technological cooperation. Furthermore, China has shown profound interest in Israel's tech sector, investing heavily in Israeli start-ups and innovation. While economic interests have primarily driven China's involvement in the region, it presents a new perspective and potential for collaboration in the Saudi-Israeli relationship. By leveraging its economic influence, China could play a significant role in mediating between the two countries, fostering an environment for dialogue and cooperation.

The European Union countries, collectively, have consistently supported the two-state solution to the Israeli-Palestinian conflict and have often pressured both Saudi Arabia and Israel to make concessions for peace. With historical ties to the region and a commitment to the values of stability, democracy, and human rights, the European countries have made diplomatic efforts to maintain dialogue and encourage rapprochement. The EU member states have been actively involved in financing projects aimed at promoting peace, stability, and economic development in the region. They have also been important trading partners for Saudi Arabia and Israel, contributing to their economic development. Their diplomatic initiatives and engagement in the region have provided an alternative perspective and have the potential for reconciliation. EU countries have also been active participants in international forums focusing on the Middle East, providing a platform for dialogue and cooperation between Saudi Arabia, Israel, and other regional actors.

The role of these global powers extends beyond direct engagement with Saudi Arabia and Israel. They also significantly influence the broader regional dynamics. Their motivations, interests, and actions heavily shape the environment in which Saudi Arabia and Israel operate, impacting the potential for normalization of relations and the prospects for lasting peace in the region.

Understanding the implications of these global powers' involvement is crucial for comprehending the wider context of Saudi-Israeli relations. Analyzing their actions, alliances, and strategies allows us to gauge the potential for collaboration, mediation, or exacerbation of tensions between Saudi Arabia and Israel. With their diverse interests and multifaceted engagement, the global powers not only impact the relationship between Saudi Arabia and Israel but contribute to shaping the future of the Middle East. Their engagement could prove instrumental in forging a stable and prosperous regional order that fosters peaceful coexistence between all stakeholders.

In a Nutshell

A. Saudi-Israeli Relations and Global Alliances

The evolving relationship between Saudi Arabia and Israel significantly impacts global alliances, particularly with the United States, which has been a key mediator in fostering closer ties between the two nations. The U.S. has offered Saudi Arabia security guarantees and advanced weapons, while pushing Israel to make meaningful concessions to the Palestinians as part of a broader deal to normalize relations. This potential normalization is seen as a strategic move to create a more integrated and stable Middle East, which aligns with U.S. interests in the region.

Furthermore, the Abraham Accords, which normalized relations between Israel and several Arab states, underscore the shifting dynamics in Middle Eastern alliances. Saudi Arabia's potential formal recognition of Israel could lead to a significant realignment, with the Saudis possibly leading other Arab and Muslim-majority countries towards normalization with Israel. This shift is partly driven by mutual interests in countering Iranian influence in the region, which has been a unifying concern for both Saudi Arabia and Israel.

B. International Reactions and Diplomatic Considerations

International reactions to the potential Saudi-Israeli normalization are mixed. While Western countries, particularly the United States, are supportive of this move as it could lead to greater stability and integration in the Middle East, other global and regional players have expressed concerns. For instance, the Palestinian Authority has been wary of these developments, fearing that their cause might be marginalized in the rush to normalize relations with Israel. The recent détente between Saudi Arabia and Iran also adds a layer of complexity, as it could shift regional power balances and influence the broader geopolitical landscape.

Countries like Russia and China are also keenly observing these developments. Russia, having a strategic interest in maintaining its influence in the Middle East, particularly in Syria, might view the closer ties between Saudi Arabia and Israel as a challenge to its interests. Conversely, China, which has recently brokered the Saudi-Iranian rapprochement, might see this as an opportunity to expand its role and influence in the region, potentially at the expense of U.S. geopolitical interests.

C. The Role of Other Global Powers

The role of other global powers, notably Russia and China, is crucial in the context of Saudi-Israeli relations. China's involvement in mediating between Saudi Arabia and Iran indicates its growing influence in Middle Eastern affairs, which could counterbalance U.S. influence in the region. This involvement is part of China's broader strategy to secure its economic interests, particularly in energy and trade routes, through diplomatic engagements rather than military interventions.

Russia, on the other hand, has been a key player in Syria and has maintained a complex relationship with both Iran and Israel. The potential Saudi-Israeli normalization might prompt Russia to recalibrate its strategies in the Middle East, especially if it leads to a weakening of Iran's regional position, which could undermine Russian interests in supporting the Assad regime in Syria.

In conclusion, the evolving Saudi-Israeli relations are set against a backdrop of shifting global alliances, with significant implications for international diplomacy. The United States plays a pivotal role as a mediator, while other global powers like Russia and China are strategically positioning themselves to respond to these changes. The outcome of these dynamics will likely reshape the geopolitical landscape of the Middle East and influence global diplomatic relations in the coming years.

Sources and References

[1] https://www.aljazeera.com/news/2017/11/21/what-is-behind-the-covert-israeli-saudi-relations

[2] https://en.wikipedia.org/wiki/Israel%E2%80%93Saudi_Arabia_relations

[3] https://www.pbs.org/newshour/show/how-normalized-relations-between-saudi-arabia-and-israel-could-change-the-middle-east

[4] https://www.brookings.edu/articles/how-to-understand-israel-and-saudi-arabias-secretive-relationship/

[5] https://www.unav.edu/en/web/global-affairs/secret-diplomacy-in-the-middle-east-negotiations-for-saudi-arabia-normalization-of-relations-with-israel

[6] https://moderndiplomacy.eu/2024/02/17/evolution-of-saudi-israel-relations-unveiling-the-shift-from-quiet-diplomacy-to-full-normalization/

[7] https://www.washingtonpost.com/business/energy/2023/09/22/a-saudi-israeli-peace-deal-who-wants-what-and-why/9284a33c-595b-11ee-bf64-cd88fe7adc71_story.html

[8] https://www.aljazeera.com/news/2023/9/21/whats-happening-with-normalising-ties-between-saudi-arabia-and-israel

[9] https://carnegieendowment.org/2020/10/15/what-would-happen-if-israel-and-saudi-arabia-established-official-relations-pub-82964

[10] https://www.fdd.org/analysis/2024/04/27/blinken-to-address-normalization-with-israel-during-visit-to-saudi-arabia/

[11] https://www.brookings.edu/articles/the-emergence-of-gcc-israel-relations-in-a-changing-middle-east/

[12] https://www.theguardian.com/world/2023/sep/21/saudi-arabia-getting-closer-to-normalising-relations-with-israel-crown-prince-says

[13] https://www.atlanticcouncil.org/blogs/menasource/saudi-arabia-israel-two-state-gaza-normalization/

[14] https://www.chathamhouse.org/publications/the-world-today/2024-02/gulf-states-have-power-revive-two-state-solution

[15] https://www.reuters.com/world/middle-east/blinken-cites-progress-with-saudis-normalising-ties-with-israel-2024-03-21/

[16] https://www.ibanet.org/article/D2659617-4CAB-4FE9-8B60-A971485EC3D6

[17] https://gulfif.org/saudi-israeli-relations-no-longer-depend-on-washington/

[18] https://www.tandfonline.com/doi/full/10.1080/03068374.2022.2134657

[19] https://www.jstor.org/stable/pdf/resrep04754.16.pdf

[20] https://www.bbc.co.uk/news/world-middle-east-42094105

IX

Societal Impact and Domestic Perspectives

Public Opinion on Saudi-Israeli Relations

The public opinion on Saudi-Israeli relations plays a central role in understanding the multifaceted societal impact of this relationship. Balancing historical narratives, religious beliefs, political ideologies, and geostrategic considerations, the public sentiment in both Saudi Arabia and Israel towards each other has been dynamic and subject to change over time.

Within Saudi Arabia, the public opinion towards Israel has traditionally been shaped by strong anti-Israeli sentiments due to the ongoing Israeli-Palestinian conflict and Israel's perceived occupation of Palestinian territories. The Saudi government's strict adherence to a non-recognition policy towards Israel has further influenced public sentiments. The Saudi media, religious leaders, and educational institutions often portray Israel as an aggressor and emphasize the importance of supporting the Palestinians' struggle for their rights and statehood.

However, recent years have witnessed notable shifts in Saudi Arabia's public opinion. The rise of Crown Prince Mohammed bin Salman and his ambitious reforms, including economic diversification and openness to foreign investments, have led to a more nuanced view towards Israel among certain segments of the population. Some younger Saudis, in particular, are more open to engaging with Israel and recognize the potential benefits of establishing diplomatic relations. Nonetheless, any potential normalization of relations remains a sensitive issue, and there is a need for cautious diplomatic efforts to address the concerns of the more conservative and religiously devout sections of society.

In Israel, public opinion towards Saudi Arabia has also evolved. The diversity of perspectives ranges from those who view Saudi Arabia as a potential ally in a volatile Middle East region to those who remain skeptical due to the country's human rights record and perceived support for extremism. With Israel facing increasing isolation in the region, some view improved relations with Saudi Arabia as an opportunity to enhance regional stability and counter common adversaries such as Iran.

The shifts in public opinion within Israel can be attributed to several factors. Firstly, the shared geostrategic concerns regarding Iran's nuclear program and regional influence have led to discreet cooperation between Israeli and Saudi security officials. To some extent, this cooperation has shaped public opinion, with proponents highlighting the benefits of a potential strategic alignment in countering common threats. Secondly, the growing normalization of relations between Israel and other Arab countries, such as the United Arab Emirates and Bahrain, has influenced public sentiment towards Saudi Arabia. Increasingly, Israelis see the potential benefits of establishing formal ties with Saudi Arabia, such as enhanced economic cooperation and shared regional security. However, it is essential to note that public discourse within Israel remains vibrant and diverse, with ongoing debates and discussions about the potential implications of closer relations with Saudi Arabia.

Cultural and Religious Implications

The cultural and religious implications of Saudi-Israeli relations are profound, considering the historical and religious connections of both nations to the region. Saudi Arabia, as the birthplace of Islam, holds tremendous religious importance, while Israel serves as the historical homeland of the Jewish people. Any engagement between these countries must navigate the sensitive religious and cultural landscapes that accompany their respective identities.

For Saudi Arabia, the religious implications of engaging with Israel are multifaceted and potentially controversial within the wider Muslim world. The role of Saudi Arabia as the custodian of the Islamic holy sites in Mecca and Medina adds layer of religious sensitivities. Historically, Saudi Arabia has positioned itself as a leader among Muslim nations, and any perceived normalization of relations with Israel would need to manage these complex dynamics carefully. The religious sentiments and unity of the Muslim community concerning the Israeli-Palestinian conflict also play a significant role in shaping Saudi society's cultural perspectives towards Israel.

Moreover, the ongoing Israeli-Palestinian conflict has long been a central component of Muslim identity and solidarity. Therefore, any shift in Saudi Arabia's position toward recognizing Israel or establishing formal diplomatic ties would need to be meticulously managed to avoid potential backlash from the broader Muslim community. Striking a balance between religious considerations and geopolitical interests remains a delicate challenge for Saudi Arabia.

In Israel, cultural and religious considerations are also essential factors to consider when contemplating closer relations with Saudi

Arabia. While Israel is predominantly a Jewish state, it is also home to significant Muslim and Christian minority populations. The potential for increased religious tourism from Saudi Arabia, if diplomatic relations were normalized, could have far-reaching impacts on both the Israeli tourism industry and the religious fabric of the country. Careful consideration of how these religious communities and their institutions will be affected is crucial in assessing the cultural implications of closer ties.

Economic Opportunities and Challenges

Given the resource-rich economies, advanced technologies, and skilled labor forces of both nations, the potential economic opportunities and challenges arising from Saudi-Israeli relations are substantial. Exploring avenues for economic cooperation becomes an important element in the overall societal impact and domestic perspectives associated with their evolving relationship.

In Saudi Arabia, the Saudi Vision 2030 plan serves as a transformative roadmap aiming to diversify the Saudi economy and reduce its dependence on oil, thus creating opportunities for partnerships with other countries. By opening up sectors such as tourism, entertainment, and renewable energy, the Saudi government seeks to attract foreign investments and expertise. As part of this plan, Israel's advanced technology sector, entrepreneurial ecosystem, and innovation-driven economy offer potential avenues for collaboration. Leveraging Israeli expertise in areas such as agritech, water management, cybersecurity, and healthcare could yield significant benefits for Saudi Arabia's economic diversification efforts.

Similarly, Israel's economy is already robust and diverse, but it could benefit from trade and investment opportunities with Saudi Arabia. The Saudi market, with its large population, offers vast potential for Israeli businesses, particularly in sectors such as agriculture, water management, cybersecurity, renewable energy, and high-tech innovation. Enhanced economic cooperation could open new markets, increase trade volumes, and foster further innovation through the exchange of knowledge and expertise between the two countries.

However, challenges exist in forging economic ties between Saudi Arabia and Israel due to the political and cultural differences between the two nations. While there is a growing understanding of the economic benefits, public sentiment, boycott movements, and potential clashes over economic policies and priorities pose obstacles. Geopolitical considerations, including ongoing regional tensions and conflicts, can also impact the pace and extent of economic cooperation. Consequently, navigating investment and trade policies in both countries requires careful diplomacy, pragmatic decision-making, and the creation of an enabling environment for business collaboration.

Despite these challenges, the potential economic partnership between Saudi Arabia and Israel remains a crucial aspect of the societal impact and domestic perspectives associated with their evolving relationship. Balancing the economic opportunities with cultural sensitivities and political realities will be essential in shaping the future trajectory of this relationship.

A. PUBLIC OPINION ON SAUDI-ISRAELI RELATIONS

Public opinion plays a crucial role in shaping the dynamics of international relations and can significantly influence the trajectory of diplomatic engagements between nations. In the case of

Saudi-Israeli relations, understanding the sentiments and attitudes of the public towards this partnership becomes essential. This chapter delves into the various aspects of public opinion concerning Saudi-Israeli relations, exploring the nuances and complexities surrounding this significant topic.

The Saudi-Israeli relationship has been historically contentious due to numerous factors, such as the ongoing Israeli-Palestinian conflict, religious differences, and regional power dynamics. These factors have inevitably shaped public opinions in both countries.

Within Saudi Arabia, the public opinion on Israel has traditionally been negative. The Israeli occupation of Palestinian territories and the mistreatment of Palestinians have deeply resonated with many Saudi citizens. The Israeli government's policies towards Palestinians are viewed as oppressive and in violation of human rights. Moreover, the Saudi population, predominantly Muslim, has strong religious ties to Jerusalem, which further implicates their sentiment towards Israel. The Al-Aqsa Mosque, located in Jerusalem, is considered the third holiest site in Islam, intensifying the emotional and religious connection between the Saudi people and the Palestinian cause.

However, there have been subtle shifts in Saudi public opinion in recent times. Under the leadership of Crown Prince Mohammed bin Salman, the government has sought to diversify and modernize the kingdom's economy, aiming to reduce its dependence on oil revenues. As part of this ambitious agenda, the Crown Prince has pursued closer ties with Israel, driven by shared geopolitical interests and economic opportunities.

While these efforts have faced resistance from conservative elements within Saudi society, who see them as compromising Palestinian rights, there is also a segment of the population that views engagement with Israel as a pragmatic move towards stability, security, and economic growth. This segment recognizes the potential for cooperation in various sectors, including technology, agriculture, water management, and counterterrorism. They believe that by leveraging Israel's technological expertise, Saudi Arabia can accelerate its economic transformation and improve its security capabilities. Furthermore, a closer relationship with Israel may create opportunities for academic and cultural exchanges, fostering mutual understanding between the two nations.

To gauge public opinion accurately, it is essential to consider the diversity within Saudi society. While most current discussions center around the views of the general public, a nuanced understanding requires examining viewpoints among different demographics, including the religious conservatives, progressives, intellectuals, and the youth. Each segment may interpret and respond to the Saudi-Israeli relationship differently, influenced by their unique experiences, values, and priorities.

The conservative elements within Saudi society, including religious clerics and activists, remain cautious and skeptical of the government's attempts at engagement with Israel. They emphasize the importance of maintaining solidarity with the Palestinian cause and advocate for a resolution to the Israeli-Palestinian conflict as a prerequisite for any normalization of relations. Additionally, they raise concerns about the potential impact on Saudi Arabia's Islamic identity and values if the partnership with Israel deepens.

In contrast, the progressive voices within Saudi Arabia see potential benefits from improved relations with Israel. They argue that distancing themselves from historical animosity and actively seeking dialogue can contribute to regional stability and promote a mutual understanding of each other's challenges. These voices advocate for separating the Palestinian cause from broader regional issues, suggesting that advancements in Saudi-Israeli relations can create a conducive environment for addressing the Israeli-Palestinian conflict more effectively.

On the other hand, public opinion in Israel towards Saudi Arabia has been more mixed. Some Israelis view Saudi Arabia as an essential potential ally in countering common regional threats, such as Iran's aggressive behavior and its pursuit of nuclear capabilities. They perceive the potential benefits of developing strategic partnerships and exploring economic opportunities with Saudi Arabia. The possibility of a united regional front against Iran's expansionist policies is considered strategically advantageous. Additionally, improved relations with Saudi Arabia could open up opportunities for Israeli businesses and technology companies, promoting economic growth and access to new markets.

However, others remain skeptical and cautious of any attempts at rapprochement with a country that has historically been at odds with Israel. These skeptics emphasize the importance of prioritizing the Israeli-Palestinian peace process and ensuring that any engagement with Saudi Arabia does not compromise Israel's long-standing commitments to its own national security and sovereignty. They argue that normalizing relations with Saudi Arabia without achieving a resolution to the Israeli-Palestinian conflict may introduce additional complexities and risks to Israel's security landscape.

It is important to consider that public opinion is not monolithic and can vary across different segments of society, including political, religious, and demographic divisions. Age, education, and political affiliation can also shape individual perspectives on Saudi-Israeli relations. For example, younger generations in both countries may be more open to exploring new possibilities for cooperation, while older generations may harbor deep-rooted skepticism based on their historical experiences and perceptions.

Moreover, media plays a significant role in shaping public opinion on this issue. State-controlled media outlets often reflect the official stances of their respective countries, promoting narratives that align with government policies. However, independent and social media platforms allow for more diverse viewpoints and debates among citizens, providing alternative perspectives that can influence public opinion.

The evolving nature of public opinion on Saudi-Israeli relations underscores the need to engage in open dialogue and foster greater understanding among the general population. As the diplomatic landscape continues to change, it becomes crucial to bridge the gap between public concerns and policymakers' decisions. Public opinion can serve as a barometer for decision-makers to gauge support or opposition to diplomatic initiatives, ensuring that any engagement with Saudi Arabia is not only driven by strategic considerations but is also aligned with the aspirations and values of the Israeli people.

In conclusion, public opinion on Saudi-Israeli relations is diverse and multifaceted. While historical and ideological factors continue to influence sentiment in both countries, there are also evolving viewpoints, driven by changing geopolitical dynamics and economic interests. Acknowledging and addressing public concerns is vital for ensuring the sustainability and effectiveness of any future diplomatic engagements between Saudi Arabia and Israel. Both countries can forge a path towards a more stable and prosperous Middle East through understanding and engaging with the complexities of public opinion.

B. CULTURAL AND RELIGIOUS IMPLICATIONS

Throughout history, culture and religion have significantly shaped societies and their relationships. Given the stark differences between these two countries, the cultural and religious implications of Saudi-Israeli relations are complex.

Cultural Differences:

1. Saudi Culture: Saudi Arabia is an Islamic country with deep-rooted traditions and conservative societal norms. The culture is influenced by Wahhabism, a strict interpretation of Sunni Islam that shapes various aspects of daily life, including gender roles, clothing, and social interactions. Gender segregation is prevalent, with public spaces and events often separated into male and female sections. Women in Saudi Arabia typically follow a dress code known as the abaya, covering their body and hair. Furthermore, strict moral codes govern social behaviors and interactions, with modesty and respect for religious customs being highly valued.
2. Israeli Culture: Israel, on the other hand, has a diverse and pluralistic society with Jewish, Muslim, Christian, and other religious communities. Jewish traditions and values shape Israeli culture, but it also embraces Western influences, secularism, and technological advancements. Unlike Saudi Arabia, Israel does not have gender segregation or stringent dress codes. Israeli society, particularly in cities like Tel Aviv, is known for its cosmopolitan and liberal attitudes, and people enjoy a wide range of personal freedoms and individual expressions.

Religious Perspectives:

1. Islam: Saudi Arabia's religious foundation is rooted in

Islam, specifically Sunni Islam. The two holiest cities in Islam, Mecca and Medina, are located in Saudi Arabia, making the country a custodian of some of the most sacred sites in the Islamic faith. There are concerns within Saudi society about establishing relations with Israel, as it has historically been viewed as an adversary due to the Israeli-Palestinian conflict. Some segments of the population see it as a betrayal of Muslim solidarity, considering the importance of the Palestinian cause and the status of Jerusalem in Islamic tradition.

2. Judaism: Israel, as a Jewish state, has a deep connection to Judaism and views itself as the homeland of the Jewish people. Jewish religious practices and traditions are embedded within Israeli society, with Hebrew being the official language and Jewish holidays observed at a national level. The relationship with Saudi Arabia presents unique challenges as Jews have historically faced discrimination in predominantly Muslim countries. The memory of past conflicts, such as the Arab-Israeli wars, and grievances can hinder the progress of mutual understanding and trust-building efforts between the two nations.

Mutual Interests and Challenges:

1. Jerusalem: The city of Jerusalem holds immense religious significance for both Muslims and Jews. It is home to the Al-Aqsa Mosque, the third holiest site in Islam, and the Western Wall, the holiest site in Judaism. Any diplomatic engagement between Saudi Arabia and Israel must grapple with the sensitive issue of Jerusalem's status, which has the potential to evoke

strong reactions from religious communities. Establishing a framework that respects the rights of all religious groups and seeks a peaceful resolution is essential for the progress of Saudi-Israeli relations.

2. Interfaith Dialogue: Despite the significant religious differences, there have been attempts to foster interfaith dialogue between Saudi Arabia and Israel, recognizing the importance of religious tolerance and understanding. Such initiatives aim to bridge cultural and religious gaps and promote peaceful coexistence. Interfaith dialogue can help dispel misconceptions, increase empathy, and enhance the prospects of sustainable peace. However, implementing and sustaining meaningful interfaith dialogue require commitment, trust-building, and a willingness to address challenging topics and historical grievances.

Gauging Public Opinion:

1. Saudi Arabia: Public opinion in Saudi Arabia regarding Israel is divided. The Israeli-Palestinian conflict and the treatment of Palestinians under Israeli occupation evoke strong emotions among Saudis, contributing to skepticism and resistance towards establishing diplomatic ties. However, there is also recognition within the population of the need for regional stability and the potential benefits of engaging with Israel. Saudi Arabia's leadership has taken steps towards cautiously normalizing relations, acknowledging the changing geopolitical landscape and the potential for cooperation in areas such as security, technology, and economy.

2. Israel: Israeli society holds diverse views on the

potential for relations with Saudi Arabia. While some believe in the diplomatic benefits and shared interests, others prioritize addressing human rights concerns and advancing the Israeli-Palestinian peace process before establishing deeper ties. Public opinion reflects an ongoing debate about the path towards achieving peace and ensuring the security of the Jewish state. Some see the normalization of relations with Saudi Arabia as a positive step towards regional stability and the recognition of Israel as a legitimate player in the Middle East.

Economic Opportunities and Challenges:

1. Cultural Exchange: The cultural exchange between Saudi Arabia and Israel can promote mutual understanding and appreciation of traditions and dismantle stereotypes. This can lead to economic collaborations in sectors such as tourism, arts, and education. Facilitating cultural exchanges can foster greater acceptance and tolerance, paving the way for more extensive economic cooperation between the two nations. Cultural events, exhibitions, and academic exchanges can enhance people-to-people interactions, creating opportunities to explore shared values and heritage.
2. Religious Tourism: For Saudis, visiting religious sites in Israel, such as Al-Aqsa Mosque, holds great religious significance. Developing tourism between the two countries could open up economic opportunities, but potential sensitivities related to the Israeli-Palestinian conflict and differing cultural norms must be taken into account. Ensuring that religious sites are respected and accessible to all visitors, regardless of their faith,

can contribute to the growth of religious tourism and generate economic benefits for both countries. Challenges also exist due to visa restrictions and potential security concerns, which need to be addressed to facilitate smoother travel between the two nations.

In sum, Saudi-Israeli relations' cultural and religious implications are significant factors shaping these countries' dynamics. Understanding and navigating these complexities is crucial for developing deeper ties and fostering regional stability. Balancing religious sensitivities, addressing cultural differences, and promoting interfaith dialogue can build a foundation of mutual respect and understanding in the pursuit of lasting peace. Cultivating economic opportunities through cultural exchange and religious tourism can further enhance cooperation and promote mutual prosperity.

C. ECONOMIC OPPORTUNITIES AND CHALLENGES

The economic dimension of Saudi-Israeli relations plays a significant role in shaping the dynamics between the two countries. The potential for economic collaboration and trade offers both opportunities and challenges for their bilateral relationship.

Trade and Investment Opportunities:
1. Diversification of Saudi Arabia's Economy: With the Saudi Vision 2030 initiative, Saudi Arabia aims to diversify its economy away from reliance on oil. Israel,

known for its innovation and advanced technology sectors, presents potential avenues for collaboration in areas such as renewable energy, agriculture, and water management. Israeli expertise in these areas can greatly assist Saudi Arabia in achieving its economic diversification objectives. The exchange of knowledge and technology can also help Saudi Arabia improve productivity and modernize key sectors of their economy.

2. Access to Gulf Markets: For Israel, building economic ties with Saudi Arabia can open doors to the broader Gulf Cooperation Council (GCC) market, comprising wealthy nations like the United Arab Emirates, Qatar, and Kuwait. This presents a significant economic opportunity for Israeli businesses and entrepreneurs to tap into a region with substantial purchasing power and a growing consumer base. Moreover, Israeli companies can benefit from partnerships with Saudi entities on joint ventures and projects within the GCC, leveraging their combined strengths and resources.

3. Expanding Trade: Establishing formal trade agreements and reducing trade barriers can facilitate the exchange of goods and services between the two countries. Increased trade volumes can benefit both economies and contribute to economic growth. It would be advantageous for Saudi Arabia and Israel to identify complementary sectors for trade, allowing each country to capitalize on their respective comparative advantages. Working towards eliminating trade barriers, streamlining customs processes, and harmonizing standards can enhance bilateral trade, making it more efficient and cost-effective for businesses.

Challenges and Obstacles:

1. Political Sensitivities: Economic cooperation between Saudi Arabia and Israel faces political sensitivities due to the unresolved Israeli-Palestinian conflict. Publicly embracing closer economic ties could lead to domestic backlash in Saudi Arabia and other Middle Eastern countries that support the Palestinian cause. Both countries must carefully navigate these sensitivities and seek to foster understanding and support for the potential benefits that economic cooperation can bring to their societies. For instance, campaigns promoting people-to-people interactions, cultural exchanges, and joint humanitarian initiatives can emphasize the positive outcomes of collaboration and help build goodwill among the respective populations.
2. Regional Rivalries: Saudi Arabia's competition with Iran for regional influence adds another layer of complexity to their economic engagement with Israel. The fear of alienating other Arab nations aligned with Iran might hinder the progress of economic collaborations. However, the shared regional threats posed by Iran's destabilizing activities can potentially serve as a catalyst for discreet economic cooperation between Saudi Arabia and Israel, driven by their common security concerns. Navigating this geopolitical challenge will require a delicate balancing act, with both countries working to establish a network of alliances and partnerships that help safeguard their mutual interests while maintaining regional stability.
3. Cultural and Regulatory Differences: Israel and Saudi Arabia have distinct cultural and regulatory frameworks. Adapting to each other's business practices,

legal systems, and customs may pose challenges for companies seeking to engage in cross-border ventures. Establishing clear guidelines, frameworks, and mechanisms to address these differences can promote smoother economic cooperation and ensure that businesses from both countries can operate efficiently and effectively. Engaging in joint training programs, knowledge-sharing initiatives, and establishing platforms for business-to-business interactions can enhance understanding and create a conducive environment for economic collaboration.

Shared Economic Initiatives:

1. Technological Cooperation: Both countries possess advanced technology sectors. Collaborating in areas such as artificial intelligence, cybersecurity, and financial technology can foster innovation and knowledge exchange, benefiting the economies of both nations. Joint research and development initiatives, technology transfer agreements, and startup incubation programs can facilitate the exchange of expertise and drive economic growth. Establishing innovation hubs or zones that encourage collaboration and investment in research and development can further accelerate the advancement of technology-driven industries in both Saudi Arabia and Israel.
2. Tourism Opportunities: The recent normalization of relations between Saudi Arabia and Israel has opened up the potential for tourism exchanges. Israel's rich historical and religious sites, coupled with Saudi Arabia's tourism sector development efforts, can attract visitors

Saudi Arabia and Israel

from both sides and contribute to job creation and economic growth. Developing joint tourism packages, promoting cultural exchange initiatives, and simplifying travel procedures can facilitate the growth of this sector. Collaborative marketing campaigns and the sharing of best practices in hospitality and tourism management can enhance the attractiveness of both countries as tourist destinations.

3. Infrastructure and Investment Projects: Joint infrastructure projects, such as transportation networks, ports, and industrial zones, can stimulate economic development and create employment opportunities for both Israelis and Saudis. Investment in shared ventures related to transportation, logistics, renewable energy infrastructure, and innovation hubs can boost both economies' connectivity, efficiency, and competitiveness. Additionally, promoting cross-border investments and providing favorable conditions for foreign direct investment can attract international capital, benefiting both Saudi Arabia and Israel. Establishing clear investment frameworks, addressing legal and regulatory hurdles, and implementing dispute resolution mechanisms can provide confidence to investors and create a conducive investment climate.

Economic opportunities and challenges in Saudi-Israeli relations are intertwined with broader geopolitical considerations. Both countries must carefully navigate these economic dimensions while considering the strategic, political, and societal implications. Success in maximizing their relationship's economic potential will require addressing hurdles, building trust, and leveraging mutual interests for the benefit of their economies, the broader Middle East region, and potentially global economic stability and prosperity.

In a Nutshell

A. Public Opinion on Saudi-Israeli Relations

Recent surveys provide a nuanced picture of Saudi public opinion regarding relations with Israel. A significant majority of Saudis, 96%, oppose normalization with Israel, particularly in light of recent conflicts such as the war in Gaza. This sentiment is strong across all age groups, contradicting earlier perceptions that younger Saudis might be more open to normalization due to less interest in the Palestinian issue. This opposition is rooted in a strong reaction to Israeli military actions and a robust support for the Palestinian cause, with a notable increase in favorable views towards Hamas among Saudis.

Despite this overwhelming opposition, there is a segment of the Saudi population, about one-third, that shows openness to business ties with Israel, particularly in sectors like technology, climate change, and water resource management. This indicates a complex societal landscape where economic pragmatism might compete with political and humanitarian concerns.

B. Cultural and Religious Implications

The cultural and religious implications of Saudi-Israeli relations are profound. Saudi Arabia, being the custodian of the two holiest sites in Islam, carries significant religious influence. The potential normalization with Israel is highly sensitive due to the religious significance of Jerusalem and the Al-Aqsa Mosque. Nearly half of the Saudi respondents in a survey emphasized the importance of securing Muslim rights at these religious sites as a condition for any formal relations with Israel.

Furthermore, there is a strong religious narrative that frames the Israeli-Palestinian conflict in terms of Islamic duty and solidarity with the Palestinian people. This narrative is deeply embedded in the Saudi public consciousness and affects how normalization is perceived. Any perceived compromise on Palestinian rights or Muslim rights in Jerusalem could lead to significant domestic backlash and affect the legitimacy of the Saudi leadership.

C. Economic Opportunities and Challenges

The economic dimension of Saudi-Israeli ties presents both opportunities and challenges. On the one hand, Saudi Arabia's Vision 2030 reform plan aims to diversify the economy away from oil dependency, and cooperation with Israel could bring advanced technology and investments in sectors like renewable energy, technology, and water management. This could significantly boost the Saudi economy and contribute to its development goals.

On the other hand, the economic benefits of normalization must be weighed against potential economic and political backlash both domestically and from other Arab and Muslim countries. The Saudi public's strong opposition to normalization, driven by the recent conflict in Gaza, suggests that moving forward with economic ties in the absence of a political resolution to the Palestinian issue could lead to instability and resistance within the kingdom.

In conclusion, the societal impact and domestic perspectives on Saudi-Israeli ties are marked by a complex interplay of strong opposition based on cultural and religious grounds, and a recognition of potential economic benefits. The Saudi leadership must navigate these dynamics carefully, balancing economic pragmatism with the deeply held convictions of its population regarding Palestine and Islamic solidarity.

Sources and References

[1] https://www.middleeastmonitor.com/20231223-poll-96-of-saudis-oppose-normalisation-with-israel/

[2] https://www.jpost.com/middle-east/article-760558

[3] https://www.washingtoninstitute.org/policy-analysis/third-saudis-want-business-israel-now-even-without-formal-ties-muslim-rights-top

[4] https://russiancouncil.ru/en/blogs/a-khalfa/evolution-of-saudiisrael-relations-unveiling-the-shift-from-quiet-dipl/

[5] https://apps.dtic.mil/sti/trecms/pdf/AD1164221.pdf

[6] https://en.wikipedia.org/wiki/Israel%E2%80%93Saudi_Arabia_relations

[7] https://www.washingtoninstitute.org/policy-analysis/new-poll-sheds-light-saudi-views-israel-hamas-war

[8] https://www.aljazeera.com/news/2023/9/21/whats-happening-with-normalising-ties-between-saudi-arabia-and-israel

[9] https://www.atlanticcouncil.org/blogs/menasource/saudi-arabia-israel-two-state-gaza-normalization/

[10] https://www.brookings.edu/articles/saudi-israeli-relations-the-curious-case-of-a-neom-meeting-denied/

[11] https://www.washingtoninstitute.org/policy-analysis/new-saudi-views-jews-and-israel

[12] https://carnegieendowment.org/2020/10/15/what-would-happen-if-israel-and-saudi-arabia-established-official-relations-pub-82964

[13] https://www.usip.org/publications/2023/09/saudi-israel-normalization-agreement-horizon

[14] https://www.jewishvirtuallibrary.org/saudi-israel-relations

[15] https://www.brookings.edu/articles/how-to-understand-israel-and-saudi-arabias-secretive-relationship/

[16] https://www.cnn.com/2023/06/19/middleeast/saudi-textbooks-israel-mime-intl/index.html

[17] https://www.meforum.org/64800/saudi-arabia-evolving-relationship-with-israel

[18] https://www.ibanet.org/article/D2659617-4CAB-4FE9-8B60-A971485EC3D6

[19] http://turkishpolicy.com/article/1167/saudi-israeli-relations-progress-risks-and-opportunities

X

Human Rights Concerns and Ethical Dilemmas

Human Rights Situation in Saudi Arabia and Israel

The examination of Saudi-Israeli relations inevitably brings attention to the human rights situations in both countries. Saudi Arabia has long faced criticism for its record on basic human rights, including freedom of speech, religion, and association. The well-documented restrictions on women's rights, such as the male guardianship system and the prohibition on female driving until recently, have raised concerns worldwide. Additionally, the treatment of dissidents and activists, including arbitrary detentions, torture allegations, and limited freedoms, have further contributed to the poor human rights record in the kingdom.

Saudi Arabia's interpretation of Islamic law, known as Sharia, has also been a contributing factor to human rights concerns. The application of strict religious codes often leads to discriminatory practices against minority groups such as religious minorities, individuals with sexual anomalies, and migrant workers. Blasphemy, apostasy, and homosexuality are criminalized, often resulting in severe punishment, including imprisonment and capital punishment.

Similarly, Israel has faced ongoing scrutiny regarding its treatment of Palestinians and the impact of its policies on human rights. The Israeli-Palestinian conflict has been a source of deep contention, with allegations of human rights violations on both sides. Criticism has been centered around issues such as the construction of Israeli settlements in the occupied territories, the construction of the separation wall, restrictive measures on movement, and the use of excessive force during protests. The treatment of Palestinian prisoners and detainees, restrictions on access to water and healthcare, and the demolition of homes have also raised significant concerns.

The situation in the Gaza Strip, where approximately two million Palestinians live under a blockade, is particularly alarming. The lack of access to basic services, high rates of unemployment, limited freedom of movement, and frequent military operations have led to dire humanitarian conditions. The Israeli military's response to protests and demonstrations near the border fence has resulted in the loss of numerous Palestinian lives, including many civilians.

Balancing Strategic Interests with Humanitarian Principles

The intertwining of strategic interests between Saudi Arabia and Israel poses a significant ethical dilemma. While both countries may have common goals in terms of regional stability and security, this cooperation can sometimes overlook human rights concerns. The dichotomy of prioritizing strategic interests over humanitarian principles raises questions about the moral compass of these nations and the international community.

Saudi Arabia's strategic partnership with the United States, particularly in terms of energy security and counterterrorism efforts, has often led to a muted response from the international community regarding its human rights abuses. The wielding of such influence has limited the willingness of global powers to exert meaningful pressure on the Kingdom to improve its rights record. Similarly, Israel's strategic importance as a democratic ally and regional stabilizer has led to protective measures by its allies, despite concerns about its treatment of Palestinians.

Considerations of national security, economic interests, and geopolitical dynamics often take precedence over human rights concerns, leading to uncomfortable alliances that can undermine ethical principles. Governments justify their actions by arguing that engagement with these countries can more effectively advance human rights through diplomatic channels rather than isolation. However, critics argue that such engagement can often result in turning a blind eye to ongoing abuses and providing tacit support to repressive regimes.

This balancing act becomes particularly challenging when powerful nations align their interests with countries known for their repressive policies. It raises questions not only about the moral responsibility of the involved nations but also the international community's role in upholding universal human rights standards.

International Criticism and Activism

The human rights situations in Saudi Arabia and Israel have not gone unnoticed by the international community. Amidst growing awareness and increasing activism, numerous organizations and individuals have called for improved human rights conditions and accountability for violations.

Non-governmental organizations (NGOs) such as Amnesty International, Human Rights Watch, and local watchdog groups play a vital role in documenting violations and advocating for change. They utilize various channels to raise awareness, pressure governments, and assist affected individuals and communities. These organizations have been instrumental in exposing human rights abuses and pushing for reforms in both Saudi Arabia and Israel.

International institutions such as the United Nations have also been engaged in monitoring and addressing human rights concerns in both countries. Special Rapporteurs appointed by the UN Human Rights Council regularly investigate violations, issue reports, and make recommendations for improvement. The Universal Periodic Review, conducted by the Human Rights Council, allows countries to assess and discuss their human rights records, allowing for scrutiny and recommendations from other states.

Individual activists, journalists, and concerned citizens worldwide have contributed to the dialogue on human rights in Saudi Arabia and Israel, utilizing social media platforms, advocacy campaigns, and public demonstrations. Their efforts have brought attention to ongoing violations and stimulated discussions about the ethics of supporting countries with poor human rights records.

Despite the push for accountability and reform, there are challenges associated with effecting change in both Saudi Arabia and Israel. Governments often react to these criticisms by dismissing them as interference in internal affairs or by resorting to repressive tactics, such as limiting freedoms of expression and suppressing dissent. Economic and political considerations can also hinder efforts to hold these nations accountable for their human rights records.

In sum, this chapter delves into the human rights concerns and ethical dilemmas inherent in the Saudi-Israeli relationship.

It provides a comprehensive analysis of the human rights situations in both countries, highlighting the restrictions on freedoms, treatment of dissidents, and discriminatory practices. Moreover, the chapter explores the challenges of balancing strategic interests with humanitarian principles and questions the moral compass of nations involved. It emphasizes the crucial role of NGOs, international institutions, and concerned individuals in advocating for accountability and improved human rights conditions. This chapter critically analyses these matters and sheds light on the complexities and moral considerations entwined in the Saudi-Israeli relationship.

A. HUMAN RIGHTS SITUATION IN SAUDI ARABIA AND ISRAEL

The human rights situation in both Saudi Arabia and Israel has been a subject of great scrutiny and debate, captivating the attention of the international community. In this extended chapter, we will delve further into the key issues and challenges faced by both nations in relation to human rights, as well as explore the international response and the role of civil society and international activism in pushing for change.

Saudi Arabia's Human Rights Record:

Saudi Arabia's human rights record has faced severe criticism for its treatment of its citizens and restrictions on civil liberties. The country operates under a strict interpretation of Islamic law, often limiting political freedoms, freedom of expression, and freedom of assembly. Dissent and criticism against the ruling regime are met with repression, surveillance, and arbitrary detention. Human rights defenders, journalists, and activists who dare to voice their concerns often face harassment, imprisonment, or exile. Moreover, the legal system in Saudi Arabia has been subject to scrutiny for its lack of due process, reliance on confession-based convictions, and absence of fair trials.

Beyond political freedoms, Saudi Arabia has also been heavily criticized for its treatment of women. For decades, women's rights in the Kingdom have been stifled by the guardianship system, which requires female citizens to obtain permission from a male guardian to travel, marry, or access certain government services. Although significant reforms have taken place in recent years, such as allowing women to drive and attend sporting events, gender inequality remains pervasive.

The Kingdom has also been accused of widespread use of torture, cruel and inhumane treatment of prisoners, and a lack of transparency in its judicial system. Furthermore, the prevalence of capital punishment, including public executions, continues to draw international condemnation and scrutiny.

Israel's Human Rights Challenges:

Israel faces a distinct set of human rights challenges primarily related to the Israeli-Palestinian conflict, a protracted and deeply complex issue. Critics argue that Israel's policies and practices in the occupied territories, including the West Bank and Gaza Strip, violate the rights of Palestinians and contribute to their continued repression.

In the occupied territories, Palestinians face various restrictions and human rights abuses. Settlement expansion, carried out by Israeli citizens in contravention of international law, has significantly limited the land available for Palestinians, leading to forced evictions, demolition of homes, and displacement. Palestinians also encounter barriers to freedom of movement, with the Israeli-controlled checkpoints and separation wall deeply impacting their daily lives, access to medical care, and economic opportunities.

The situation in Gaza is particularly dire, with a decade-long blockade that has severely limited the movement of goods and people, plunging the population into a humanitarian crisis. The lack of access to clean water, electricity, and healthcare exacerbates the suffering of the people and violates their fundamental rights.

Moreover, Israel's policy of administrative detention, which allows for the imprisonment of Palestinians without charge or trial, has been widely criticized by human rights organizations for denying individuals their right to a fair trial and due process.

International Response and Diplomatic Pressure:

The international community has repeatedly expressed concerns about the human rights situation in both Saudi Arabia and Israel. Various human rights organizations, such as Amnesty International and Human Rights Watch, have documented and reported on the violations and shortcomings in both countries, providing vital information for policymakers, researchers, and activists.

However, despite the overwhelming evidence, the response from the international community has varied based on geopolitical considerations, strategic alliances, and economic interests.

In the case of Saudi Arabia, Western countries have often balanced their criticisms with maintaining favorable relations due to Saudi Arabia's significant oil reserves, its influential position in the Gulf region, and regional security interests. Nonetheless, a growing international push for accountability has emerged in recent years, particularly following the murder of journalist Jamal Khashoggi in

2018, prompting countries to reconsider their approach towards Saudi Arabia's human rights violations.

The international response to Israel has been similarly complex. The Israeli-Palestinian conflict is a highly polarized issue, and many countries have found it challenging to navigate the delicate dynamics surrounding it, often restraining their criticism or expressing concerns through diplomatic channels. However, a global coalition of activists, academics, and civil society organizations has consistently advocated for Palestinian rights, leading to a growing movement for justice and accountability.

Balancing Strategic Interests and Human Rights:

Striking a balance between promoting human rights and pursuing strategic interests remains one of the greatest challenges for the international community. In the context of the Middle East, stability, security concerns, and regional dynamics often take precedence, sometimes overshadowing human rights considerations.

Countries around the world frequently find themselves grappling with the dilemma of ensuring strategic relationships while addressing human rights concerns. This balance is particularly evident in the case of Saudi Arabia, which has played a crucial role in regional security and countering terrorism.

Similarly, Israel's strategic importance as a U.S. ally, its technological advancements, and its shared security interests with various countries further complicate the response to its human rights challenges.

Role of Civil Society and International Activism:

Despite the intricacies surrounding the international response, civil society organizations and activists play a pivotal role in advocating for human rights in both Saudi Arabia and Israel.

In Saudi Arabia, a growing movement of activists and human rights defenders has been working tirelessly to expose human rights violations, seek justice for victims, and push for systemic reforms. In recent years, women's rights activists, in particular, have gained international attention for their work challenging discriminatory laws and practices.

In Israel, various civil society organizations, both Israeli and Palestinian, work tirelessly to document human rights abuses, protect the rights of vulnerable communities, and provide legal assistance to individuals affected by the conflict. They play a crucial role in raising awareness both locally and internationally, challenging oppressive policies, and seeking justice and accountability.

Beyond national borders, international activism has also played a vital role in addressing human rights challenges in both countries. Global campaigns, such as the Boycott, Divestment, and Sanctions (BDS) movement, have aimed to put economic pressure on Israel to end its occupation and respect the rights of Palestinians. Similarly, international pressure and initiatives have focused on holding Saudi Arabia accountable for its human rights violations, leading to increased scrutiny and potential repercussions.

Ultimately, the human rights situation in Saudi Arabia and Israel remains an ongoing concern that demands global attention and action. Both nations face critical challenges, whether related to political freedoms, women's rights, or the consequences of the Israeli-Palestinian conflict. Balancing strategic interests with human rights considerations continues to pose a complex dilemma for the international community. However, civil society organizations and international activism continue to champion human rights, exposing violations, pushing for justice, and working towards a more just and equitable future for all.

B. BALANCING STRATEGIC INTERESTS WITH HUMANITARIAN PRINCIPLES

In the complex realm of international relations, the challenge of balancing strategic interests with humanitarian principles poses a significant and multifaceted dilemma. This chapter delves into the intricate dynamics of Saudi-Israeli relations, where the need to safeguard national security, foster regional stability, and achieve geopolitical objectives often clashes with the imperative of upholding human rights and humanitarian values.

At its core, the Saudi-Israeli relationship is driven by shared strategic interests rooted in the volatile Middle Eastern landscape. Both countries face common threats such as extremist ideologies, terrorism, and the expanding regional influence of Iran. Recognizing the need for collaboration, Saudi Arabia and Israel have cautiously engaged in discreet cooperation, driven by the mutual recognition that their strategic objectives align. This cooperation is particularly evident in intelligence-sharing, joint military exercises, and counterterrorism efforts, all aimed at countering common adversaries and ensuring the preservation of their respective national security interests.

However, this alliance of convenience faces considerable ethical challenges stemming from the divergent human rights records of Saudi Arabia and Israel. Saudi Arabia has been widely criticized for its treatment of dissidents, restrictions on freedom of expression, violations of women's rights, and the devastating impact of its military campaign in Yemen. Similarly, Israel has faced international condemnation for its policies towards Palestinians, including the construction of settlements, restrictions on movement, and the handling of the Gaza Strip. These human rights concerns have strained their diplomatic relationships with other nations and raised profound ethical dilemmas in their pursuit of strategic objectives.

Navigating the delicate balance between strategic interests and humanitarian principles necessitates careful consideration and a nuanced approach. To address this predicament, both Saudi Arabia and Israel must prioritize dialogue and engagement, both domestically and internationally. Constructive discussions that foster a culture of respect for human rights can help raise awareness and promote positive change within society. Civil society organizations, non-governmental organizations, and individuals can play a crucial role in advocating for human rights within these countries, pushing for reforms and accountability.

International pressure and scrutiny also play a vital role in influencing the behavior of states. The global community must hold both Saudi Arabia and Israel accountable for their human rights records, urging them to adhere to international standards and remedies for violations. Diplomatic dialogue must encompass discussions on human rights concerns, creating an environment where strategic interests and humanitarian principles can be openly addressed. This includes leveraging economic ties, diplomatic engagements, and multilateral frameworks to incentivize positive change.

The alignment of strategic interests and humanitarian principles can be a daunting process, particularly when it comes to addressing the complex Israeli-Palestinian conflict. Saudi Arabia, while discreetly engaging with Israel to counter shared threats, must also ensure that its actions do not undermine the rights and aspirations of the Palestinian people. Balancing these considerations requires Saudi Arabia to actively pursue a dual-track approach: engaging in dialogue and cooperation with Israel for shared objectives, while simultaneously promoting Palestinian rights and supporting the establishment of an independent and viable Palestinian state.

Similarly, Israel must prioritize human rights and demonstrate a commitment to resolving the Israeli-Palestinian conflict through peaceful means. Recognizing the impact of its actions on the lives of Palestinians, Israel should work towards lifting restrictions on movement, halting settlement constructions, and establishing a more equitable framework for addressing the needs and aspirations of both Israelis and Palestinians. Additionally, Israel should seek meaningful engagement with moderate Arab nations like Saudi Arabia to foster a comprehensive regional peace and address deep-rooted grievances.

Finding a comprehensive and sustainable balance between strategic interests and humanitarian principles is a long-term endeavor. It requires ongoing dialogue, collaborative efforts, and a commitment to promoting positive change. Government entities, civil society organizations, and individuals should work together to develop and implement human rights mechanisms, policies, and institutions that help mitigate the ethical challenges the Saudi-Israeli relationship faces while working towards regional stability and security.

Furthermore, advancing the cause of human rights requires addressing the root causes of conflicts and instability in the region. By addressing socio-economic inequalities, political grievances, and historical tensions, Saudi Arabia and Israel can work towards building a more inclusive and tolerant society. Engaging with neighboring states and other regional actors in diplomatic initiatives and confidence-building measures can promote cooperation and alleviate human rights concerns.

In conclusion, the delicate balance between strategic interests and humanitarian principles poses an enduring challenge for Saudi-Israeli relations. While both countries must navigate this dilemma, it is essential to prioritize human rights, promote a culture of respect, and ensure accountability. Through ongoing commitment, meaningful engagement, international pressure, and comprehensive reforms, there is potential for progress in addressing these ethical challenges and forging a more balanced approach. Ultimately, the aspiration should be to achieve a symbiotic relationship where strategic interests and humanitarian principles complement each other, leading to greater regional stability, security, and respect for human rights.

C. INTERNATIONAL CRITICISM AND ACTIVISM

International criticism and activism play a crucial and multifaceted role in shaping and influencing the Saudi-Israeli relationship. Both countries face diverse criticism from various international actors and organizations due to their respective human rights records, regional policies, and geopolitical interests.

Criticism of Saudi Arabia primarily stems from concerns over its human rights practices, such as restrictions on freedom of speech, association, and religion. The country's treatment of women, activists, religious minorities, and dissidents has been widely scrutinized by international human rights organizations and governments. The Saudi government's involvement in the ongoing conflict in Yemen, including alleged war crimes and violations of humanitarian law, has further fueled international criticism. Moreover, the murder of journalist Jamal Khashoggi at the Saudi consulate in Istanbul in 2018 added to the scrutiny and raised questions about Saudi Arabia's commitment to human rights and rule of law.

This sustained criticism has the potential to impact the Saudi-Israeli relationship. It raises concerns about the compatibility of shared values and norms, specifically in terms of human rights and democratic principles. Aligning closely with a country that faces such extensive international criticism on these issues could expose Saudi Arabia to reputational risks and undermine its efforts to cultivate a positive image on the global stage. Consequently, the Saudi government may face pressure from its own population, international partners, and civil society to address these concerns before deepening ties with Israel.

Similarly, Israel has faced a significant amount of criticism and condemnation for its policies towards Palestinians, particularly in the occupied territories. Israel's settlement expansion, security measures, and military operations in Gaza have been widely criticized for their impact on Palestinian rights, freedom, and livelihoods. International human rights organizations, governments, and civil society advocate for the rights of Palestinians and for a just and lasting solution to the Israeli-Palestinian conflict. This criticism creates public relations challenges for Israel, as it raises concerns about the country's commitment to international law, human rights, and the principles of self-determination.

The Israeli government faces pressure to address international criticism and improve its image in order to strengthen its relationship with Saudi Arabia or other Arab states. This pressure is particularly relevant within the context of the Israeli-Palestinian conflict, as many Arab countries condition the normalization of ties on advancements in the peace process and a resolution to the Palestinian issue. Consequently, Israel may be compelled to review its policies, engage in dialogue, and make concessions in order to alleviate international criticism and pave the way for closer relations with Saudi Arabia.

International activism also plays a significant role in shaping the Saudi-Israeli relationship. Pro-Palestinian and human rights organizations, as well as grassroots movements, exert pressure on both governments through advocacy campaigns, boycotts, divestment initiatives, and protests. These forms of activism seek to raise awareness about perceived injustices, violations, and human rights abuses committed by both Saudi Arabia and Israel. They also aim to mobilize public opinion, governments, and international bodies to pressure the two countries for policy changes and greater accountability.

Additionally, international actors such as the United Nations, European Union, and the United States actively engage in the Saudi-Israeli relationship. They often moderate diplomatic efforts, exert diplomatic pressure, or provide financial and military support to either country. These international actors influence the dynamics between Saudi Arabia and Israel, shaping the possibilities and limitations of their engagement. Furthermore, regional powers such as Iran and Turkey actively involve themselves in the Saudi-Israeli relationship, either as critics or supporters, further complicating the geopolitical landscape.

Managing international criticism and activism poses challenges for both Saudi Arabia and Israel. They must carefully navigate the delicate balance between addressing legitimate concerns the international community raises and maintaining their national interests and security imperatives. It requires a nuanced approach, as both countries face complex political and regional contexts that shape their policy decisions. In some instances, both Saudi Arabia and Israel have taken steps towards addressing these criticisms, such as implementing internal reforms or engaging in diplomatic initiatives to promote a positive image internationally.

However, the impact of international criticism and activism on the Saudi-Israeli relationship is multi-dimensional and not easily predictable. While such criticism and activism may hinder direct diplomatic engagement and public normalization, it also creates opportunities for dialogue, transparency, and accountability. Both Saudi Arabia and Israel have a vested interest in managing these external pressures effectively, so as to navigate the complexities of their relationship while balancing their national interests, regional alliances, and global reputations.

In conclusion, international criticism and activism significantly influence the Saudi-Israeli relationship, shaping the potential for closer ties, the perception of shared values, and the progressive realization of human rights in the region. The sustained scrutiny over human rights practices, as well as the complexities of the Israeli-Palestinian conflict, pose challenges for both countries. They must carefully navigate these external pressures while considering their geopolitical interests, regional security concerns, and domestic priorities. The ability to address international criticism and activism effectively will be pivotal in shaping the future trajectory of the Saudi-Israeli relationship in an increasingly interconnected world.

In a Nutshell

A. Human Rights Situation in Saudi Arabia and Israel

Saudi Arabia

Saudi Arabia's human rights record has been widely criticized for various violations. The country has been scrutinized for its treatment of human rights defenders, activists, and dissidents, who often face arrest, lengthy prison terms, and even the death penalty for exercising their rights to freedom of expression or association. Women's rights have also been a significant concern, despite some reforms; women continue to face systemic discrimination. Migrant workers in Saudi Arabia report abuse and exploitation, and the kafala (visa sponsorship) system has been particularly criticized for giving employers excessive control over workers' mobility and legal status.

The Specialized Criminal Court (SCC) in Saudi Arabia, which was established to try terror-related crimes, has been used to sentence individuals to lengthy prison terms following grossly unfair trials for peaceful activities such as online speech. The country's human rights dialogue with the EU and other international actors has often been criticized for not leading to substantial improvements on the ground.

Israel

Israel has faced international criticism for its treatment of Palestinians, both within its borders and in the occupied territories. Human rights organizations have reported on a range of violations, including unlawful killings, excessive use of force, forced displacement, and restrictions on movement and access to services. The blockade of the Gaza Strip has been described as a form of collective punishment and a serious violation of international humanitarian law.

During the 2021 conflict, Israeli authorities were accused of crimes against humanity, including apartheid and persecution, due to discriminatory policies and practices that privilege Jewish Israelis over Palestinians. The United Nations has called for accountability and justice for violations by all parties in the Occupied Palestinian Territories (OPT) and Israel, emphasizing the need for investigations into violations.

B. Balancing Strategic Interests with Humanitarian Principles

The relationship between Saudi Arabia and Israel is complex, with both countries facing significant human rights challenges. Balancing strategic interests with humanitarian principles is a delicate task for both nations and the international community.

Saudi Arabia's strategic interests included, until recently, maintaining regional stability, countering Iranian influence, and pursuing economic modernization under Vision 2030. However, the kingdom's human rights record challenges its international reputation and relations with Western allies.

Israel's strategic interests involve ensuring national security, maintaining regional alliances, and seeking broader acceptance in the Islamic world. Yet, its policies towards Palestinians and the ongoing conflict in Gaza have led to international condemnation and strained relations with some countries.

Both countries must navigate the tension between their strategic objectives and the imperative to adhere to humanitarian principles. This includes respecting human rights, ensuring accountability for violations, and engaging in meaningful dialogue to address the underlying causes of conflict and repression.

C. International Criticism and Activism

International criticism of Saudi Arabia and Israel's human rights records has been persistent. Human rights organizations, the United Nations, and some countries have called for accountability and reforms. Activists and NGOs continue to document violations and advocate for the rights of affected populations.

In Saudi Arabia, international actors have urged the kingdom to release political prisoners, end the death penalty, and reform the kafala system. The European Parliament and the US have taken steps to address human rights concerns, but these efforts have often been criticized as insufficient.

In Israel, international organizations have called for an end to the blockade of Gaza, the cessation of settlement activities, and respect for the rights of Palestinians. The international community has also been urged to support a just and lasting solution to the Israel-Palestine conflict that upholds the rights and dignity of all people involved. An international judicial investigation has been initiated into an Israeli genocide in Gaza.

In both cases, international activism is crucial in highlighting human rights issues and pressuring governments to make positive changes. However, the effectiveness of these efforts is often limited by geopolitical considerations and the strategic interests of powerful states.

Sources and References

[1] https://apnews.com/article/saudi-arabia-un-human-rights-council-2098e8faa0dd947157bd2ef1398a9737
[2] https://www.amnesty.org.uk/saudi-arabia-human-rights-raif-badawi-king-salman
[3] https://en.wikipedia.org/wiki/Human_rights_in_Saudi_Arabia
[4] https://www.hrw.org/report/2021/04/27/threshold-crossed/israeli-authorities-and-crimes-apartheid-and-persecution
[5] https://www.thehindu.com/news/international/saudi-arabia-hears-dozens-of-countries-critique-its-human-rights-record-at-the-un-in-geneva/article67768676.ece
[6] https://www.hrw.org/world-report/2024/country-chapters/saudi-arabia
[7] https://www.aljazeera.com/news/2023/9/21/whats-happening-with-normalising-ties-between-saudi-arabia-and-israel
[8] https://en.wikipedia.org/wiki/Human_rights_in_Israel
[9] https://www.amnesty.org/en/location/middle-east-and-north-africa/middle-east/saudi-arabia/report-saudi-arabia/
[10] https://carnegieendowment.org/2023/11/17/arab-peace-initiative-ii-how-arab-leadership-could-design-peace-plan-in-israel-and-palestine-pub-91047
[11] https://www.iai.it/en/pubblicazioni/saudi-arabias-balancing-game-palestinian-cause-and-regional-leadership
[12] https://www.atlanticcouncil.org/blogs/menasource/saudi-arabia-israel-two-state-gaza-normalization/
[13] https://www.ohchr.org/en/press-releases/2024/02/un-report-calls-accountability-justice-violations-all-parties-opt-and-israel
[14] https://www.hrw.org/world-report/2023/country-chapters/saudi-arabia

[15] https://www.ohchr.org/en/press-releases/2024/02/israelopt-un-experts-appalled-reported-human-rights-violations-against

[16] https://en.wikipedia.org/wiki/Human_rights_violations_against_Palestinians_by_Israel

[17] https://www.amnesty.org/en/location/middle-east-and-north-africa/report-middle-east-and-north-africa/

[18] https://www.hrw.org/world-report/2022/country-chapters/saudi-arabia

[19] https://www.brookings.edu/articles/how-to-understand-israel-and-saudi-arabias-secretive-relationship/

XI

Conclusion

Throughout this book, we have delved into the intricate and often clandestine relationship between Saudi Arabia and Israel, endeavoring to unravel the multifaceted tapestry of their interactions. This relationship, cloaked in secrecy, has deep historical roots and is shrouded by complex geopolitical considerations, regional dynamics, and conflicting interests. As such, it holds significant implications for the Middle East and the broader domain of global diplomacy.

Both Saudi Arabia and Israel have a long and complex history in the Middle East, shaped by unique circumstances and regional challenges. Saudi Arabia, as the birthplace of Islam and custodian of the two holiest sites in Islam, holds a significant role within the Arab and Muslim world. Its historic support for the Palestinian cause and its leadership position in the Gulf Cooperation Council (GCC) have traditionally dictated its approach to Israel. Conversely, Israel, as the world's only Jewish state built on an Arab land after dispossessing its people, emerged from the Zionist movement's aspirations for a homeland following World War II. Born out of a vision for

Zionist self-determination, it faced hostility and opposition from many Arab states, including Saudi Arabia.

Historically, Saudi-Israeli relations have undergone numerous shifts and transformations. While ties were initially non-existent, early encounters between Saudi rulers and Zionist leaders during the early 20th century showcased glimpses of a potential relationship. However, the emergence of the Arab-Israeli conflict and the Israeli Occupation in 1948 created an insurmountable hurdle that strained relations for decades to come. Saudi Arabia, along with other Arab states, supported the Palestinian cause and withheld recognition of Israel, reinforced by the Arab League's collective stance on the Israeli-Palestinian conflict.

Within this context, the clandestine cooperation between Saudi Arabia and Israel would seem sinful if we consider the Saudi-Wahhabi traditional worldview. Yet, throughout the years, both countries acknowledged the existence of common interests and mutual concerns, particularly in the face of regional threats. Covert communication channels, encouraged and sponsored by the USA, were established during the Cold War, as Saudi and Israeli officials recognized the need for discreet collaboration. While the specifics and extent of such cooperation remain largely hidden from public view, evidence suggests that intelligence sharing, counterterrorism efforts, and defense collaborations have taken place discreetly over the years.

The shared regional challenges and geopolitical landscape have further propelled the Saudi-Israeli relationship forward. The rise of extremist groups such as Al-Qaeda, the Taliban, and more recently, the Islamic State (ISIS), coupled with ongoing sectarian tensions, have posed grave threats to both Saudi Arabia and Israel. Covert cooperation in intelligence and counterterrorism efforts has played an instrumental role in sharing information, preemptively countering terrorist plots, and maintaining regional stability.

Economic collaborations and trade agreements have also played a significant role in the Saudi-Israeli relationship. Despite the absence of official diplomatic ties, both countries have gradually established economic connections and explored trade opportunities. Over the years, bilateral trade has grown, encompassing various sectors such as technology, agriculture, and security equipment. Moreover, Israeli innovation and technological advancements have attracted the attention of Saudi Arabian officials, who increasingly recognize the potential benefits and mutual gains of increased economic engagements with Israel.

However, it is important to note that the Arab-Israeli conflict has consistently challenged the Saudi-Israeli relationship. Arab public opinion, fueled by historical grievances and solidarity with the Palestinian cause, has created a substantial barrier to open diplomatic relations. Saudi Arabia, as a prominent Arab and Muslim nation, must carefully navigate these sentiments and the broader geopolitical implications. However, recent geopolitical developments, particularly the shared concerns over Iran's regional ambitions and its destabilizing activities, have facilitated a shift in the Saudi stance towards Israel.

The Saudi-Iran rivalry and Israel's strategic position in the region have created unique opportunities for closer ties and cooperation. Behind closed doors, Saudi Arabia has softened its rhetoric towards Israel, recognizing its role as a regional power and a potential ally in addressing broader challenges facing the Middle East. The shared perception of Iran as a common adversary has fostered discrete diplomatic, security, and intelligence collaborations on a broader scale.

Looking ahead, the future prospects for Saudi-Israeli relations are both promising and challenging. While the potential for diplomatic open ties exists, several obstacles must be navigated. Deep-seated historical animosities, divergent regional interests, and domestic political pressures complicate the road to normalization.

Additionally, the ongoing Arab-Israeli conflict, coupled with popular sentiment and public opinion throughout the Muslim world, poses significant hurdles to the establishment of full diplomatic ties.

Yet, despite these challenges, the shifting geopolitical landscape and the imperative to confront common threats may lead to a gradual and cautious rapprochement between Saudi Arabia and Israel. Regional dynamics and evolving alliances in the Middle East, including the Abraham Accords between Israel and several Arab nations, may provide a platform for advancing further cooperation between Saudi Arabia and Israel. Building trust through incremental steps, track-two diplomacy initiatives, and discreet diplomatic contacts could contribute to a more comprehensive engagement in the future.

The societal impact and domestic perspectives surrounding Saudi-Israeli relations also warrant consideration. Public opinion on the relationships between both countries, influenced by cultural, religious, and historical factors, plays a significant role in shaping the trajectory of engagement. Throughout the Muslim world, solidarity with the Palestinian cause and anti-Israel sentiment often shape the perception of Saudi-Israeli relations. Saudi Arabia's ability to align its national and regional interests with public sentiment remains crucial in navigating this complex landscape.

Furthermore, economic opportunities and challenges must be carefully weighed. Increased trade and investment between Saudi Arabia and Israel offer potential benefits for both countries, fostering economic growth, technological exchange, and job creation. However, concerns regarding dependence, competition, and structural imbalances must also be addressed to ensure long-term benefits for both economies.

Finally, it is imperative to acknowledge the human rights concerns and ethical dilemmas inherent within both Saudi Arabia and Israel. As we examine the complexities of their relationship, it becomes apparent that balancing strategic interests with humanitarian principles presents a complex task, demanding careful consideration and ethical reflection. International criticism and activism have brought attention to these concerns, highlighting the need for transparency, accountability, and ongoing efforts to effect positive change within both nations.

In conclusion, this extended exploration has comprehensively analysed the behind-the-scenes Saudi-Israeli relationship, untangling its historical context, contemporary dynamics, and future prospects. By comprehending the intricate nature of this relationship, leveraging its potential for peace, stability, and prosperity becomes more feasible. As the geopolitical landscape continues to evolve, understanding the nuances and complexities of Saudi-Israeli relations is essential in navigating the Middle East's intricate web of diplomacy and regional dynamics.

Last but not least, no peace accords in the Middle East will be sustainable if many regional players (Palestinians, Iranians, Yemenis, etc.) are unsatisfied or resent the accords as hostile to their interests. Therefore, it is wise to have a broad picture of all the challenges that could spoil the Saudi-Israeli honeymoon if they occurred at the expense of those players.

A. SUMMARY OF KEY FINDINGS

Since the establishment of their respective states, Saudi Arabia and Israel have maintained a complex and often secretive relationship. Allegedly, under the surface of official Arab policies that have resisted recognizing Israel's existence, discreet cooperation and contacts have evolved, shaped by shared interests and geopolitical realities. This chapter aims to delve deeper into the intricacies of this relationship, exploring key historical developments, underlying factors, and future prospects.

Historical Developments:

The origins of Saudi-Israeli relations can be traced back to the aftermath of the 1973 Arab-Israeli War, also known as the Yom Kippur War. The war highlighted the inadequacy of Arab military capabilities and led to Saudi Arabia reassessing its approach toward Israel. In the years following the war, Saudi Arabia, as one of the leading Arab states, began exploring covert channels of communication with Israeli officials.

While public recognition of contact remained limited, behind-the-scenes cooperation was reportedly initiated by Prince Fahd, who later became King Fahd. Through discreet meetings, Saudi officials and Israeli counterparts discussed shared concerns, including combating the rise of radical ideologies, countering Soviet influence in the region, and addressing the common threat posed by Iran's Islamic Revolution.

During the 1980s, as the Soviet Union's influence in the Middle East waned, Saudi Arabia and Israel found common ground in countering regional destabilization. While still refraining from official diplomatic relations, there were indications of increased intelligence exchanges and security cooperation. This period marked a turning point in Saudi-Israeli relations, as both countries recognized the strategic benefits of discreet collaboration.

Underlying Factors:

Several factors have shaped and continue to shape the Saudi-

Israeli relationship. First and foremost, the perceived Iranian threat looms large in the minds of both Saudi Arabia and Israel. The Iranian Revolution of 1979, followed by Iran's expansionist ambitions and its support for proxy groups across the region, fueled concerns about regional stability and Shiite dominance. As a result, Saudi Arabia and Israel have found common ground in their opposition to Iranian influence, leading to greater covert cooperation.

Furthermore, the persistent Arab-Israeli conflict has compelled regional powers to recalibrate their positions and alliances. In recent years, a convergence of interests between Saudi Arabia and Israel has emerged, driven by the perception of shared threats posed by non-state actors like Hezbollah and Hamas, as well as the spread of extremist ideologies. Recognizing the limitations of traditional Arab alliances, Saudi Arabia has acknowledged Israel's strong military capabilities and its potential to contribute to regional security.

Another factor influencing Saudi-Israeli relations is the changing dynamics within Saudi society itself. Crown Prince Mohammed bin Salman's Vision 2030 and his efforts to modernize the country have sparked a broader societal debate, including discussions on the kingdom's relationship with Israel. The younger generation of Saudis, exposed to global perspectives and influenced by social media, has shown a greater willingness to engage in dialogue with Israelis and challenge the traditional narratives regarding Israel.

Future Prospects and Challenges:

The future prospects for Saudi-Israeli relations hold both promise and challenges. While there have been recent indications of warming ties, the road to official normalization is laden with obstacles. Public opinion remains a significant hurdle, as anti-Israel sentiments are deeply ingrained in Arab societies. Any overt rapprochement would require carefully managing public perception, providing reassurances regarding Palestinian rights, and navigating religious sensitivities.

Furthermore, the Israeli-Palestinian conflict remains a central obstacle to widespread Arab recognition of Israel. While Saudi Arabia has shown willingness to engage in indirect talks and peace initiatives, a comprehensive resolution to the conflict is necessary to unlock the potential for Saudi-Israeli normalization fully.

The involvement of global powers, such as the United States, also shapes the trajectory of this relationship. The evolving dynamics of the Middle East and the reconfiguration of regional alliances necessitate recalibrations in Saudi Arabia's foreign policy. As the United States seeks to build a coalition against Iran, it has encouraged closer ties between Saudi Arabia and Israel, creating opportunities for increased cooperation.

However, ethical dilemmas and human rights concerns must not be overlooked. Saudi Arabia and much more Israel - which committed another genocide in Gaza - face criticism for their domestic records, raising questions about the balance between strategic interests and humanitarian principles. International pressure, activism, and the role of civil society play vital roles in shaping the discourse surrounding Saudi-Israeli relations.

Economic considerations also contribute to the evolving relationship. Both Saudi Arabia and Israel recognize the potential for economic collaboration, particularly in technology, agriculture, and water resource management sectors.

Moreover, the energy landscape further influences the Saudi-Israeli relationship. As a major oil-producing country, Saudi Arabia significantly influences global energy markets. On the other hand, Israel has made notable strides in renewable energy technologies.

IN A NUTSHELL

> ALL THE PREVIOUSLY MENTIONED COMMON INTERESTS THROUGHOUT THE BOOK DO NOT WEIGH A LOT AGAINST THE GENOCIDE THAT OCCURRED IN GAZA.
> WITHOUT A REAL SOLUTION FOR THE PALESTINIAN PLIGHT, WITHOUT AN INDEPENDENT AND SOVEREIGN INTERNATIONALLY RECOGNIZED PALESTINIAN STATE ON THE PRE-1967 BORDERS (*ACCORDING TO THE UN 1947 PARTITION, NOT THE 6-DAY WAR*), THERE IS NO POSSIBLE PEACE AND NO POSSIBLE STABILITY FOR THE REGION. ISRAEL WILL NEVER BE ABLE TO HAVE SECURITY INSIDE THE TERRITORIES IT

HAS OCCUPIED SINCE 1967 AND EVEN INSIDE THE 1948 "STATE" IT HAS DECLARED. THE 7 OCTOBER HAMAS ATTACK MADE THE EVIDENCE. AND IF, DESPITE ALL WISDOM, SAUDI ARABIA DECIDED TO FALL BLINDLY INTO THE US-ISRAELI TRAP AND GOT TIED UP TO A MURDEROUS AND FASCIST ISRAEL, IT WILL ALSO NEVER HAVE PEACE, SECURITY AND STABILITY. NOR WOULD IT BE ACCEPTED AS AN ARAB AND MUSLIM LEADER ANYMORE.

THE SAUDI-ISRAELI RELATIONSHIP IS DOOMED TO FAIL WITHOUT A SOLUTION FOR THE PALESTINIANS, AND SUCH IS THE CASE OF ALL THE LAMENTABLE AND PROVISORY "PEACE ACCORDS" BETWEEN THE ISRAELI COLONISATION ENTITY AND OTHER ARAB STATES.

www.ingramcontent.com/pod-product-compliance
Lightning Source LLC
Chambersburg PA
CBHW051540020426
42333CB00016B/2025